editor assistant: Stéphane Argillet

Special Thanks to :
Alban Barré, Marianne Min, Andrew Rothwell

© Éditions Dis Voir

3, rue Beautreillis

75004 Paris

ISBN 2-906-571-76-8

PRINTED IN EUROPE

this series edited by
DANIÈLE RIVIÈRE

in the same serie

SOUND AND THE VISUAL ARTS
Jean-Yves Bosseur
IN FAVOUR OF TODAY'S ART
François Dagognet
CLEMENT GREENBERG BETWEEN THE LINES
Thierry de Duve

MULTIPLE MEANING

TECHNO:

AN ARTISTIC AND POLITICAL
LABORATORY OF THE PRESENT

MICHEL GAILLOT

MULTIPLE MEANING

TECHNO:

AN ARTISTIC AND POLITICAL
LABORATORY OF THE PRESENT

translated from the French by
Warren Niesluchowski

CONTENTS

Acknowledgments

I wish to thank Jean-Luc Nancy and Michel Maffesoli for the interviews they so generously accorded me,
as well as Sylvie Blocher, Maria Spangaro, and Célia Izoard for their help and support.

Our heritage is preceded by no testament.
—René Char

We can repose on nothing.
But only on ourselves.
A comic responsibility is incumbent on us and weighs us down.
Until our own time men reposed after each thing, one on the other—or on God.
—Georges Bataille

Foreword

*T*hese lines will no doubt run through too many different fields of investigation not to incur legitimate criticism on the part of well-informed specialists. Thus the philosopher, sociologist, musicologist, critic, or historian will certainly remain unsatisfied. Those who hope to find an exhaustive description of either techno music or contemporary art will also be *deçus*, as we say in French, both disappointed and deceived. We attempt more modestly to convey some of their general features, as well as to indicate certain common tendencies which may lead to exchange and mutual explanation.

Our purpose is neither to idealize techno, defend it, nor one way or another make it a model for contemporary art, but rather to show, based only on techno and what it manifests, politically or artistically, how that which makes it what is also concerns, or rather contaminates, the present-day domains of both art and politics, to the point where there is no doubt they now form but one space. By virtue of an increasing cross-breeding or hybridization, they have been weaving together new forms of sharing. These ever-moving forms are more ephemeral, and a factual belonging to a State, Nation, or Ideology gives way to a multiplicity of elective communities which no longer repose on some Meaning or Truth to be represented, appropriated, or prophesied. But one cannot expect of this fecund cross-breeding that it give birth to a new Ideal on which the possibility of either a communitarian esthetics (an estheticizing of the political) or an esthetic community (a politicizing of art) might be reactivated. Quite the contrary, we shall attempt to show how in our time the historical figures of this Ideal and its various ideological declensions have exhausted (and continue to exhaust) themselves, and how this exhaustion has opened up new areas of singular and collective experience, of which techno has in some way been an outpost. In the global vacillation of markers that still allows some 'moderns' to fashion an art and politics based on some one-and-only Truth, techno seems to us to be a 'laboratory of our present,' a present that allows for no postponement and demands of us that we learn how to come up with new ways of sharing and possession in common.

To sum up, basing ourselves on the characteristics proper to movements in popular culture (the pre-eminence of the body, and, in general, of the festive, the replacement of a logic of representation by a logic of participation, the broadening of the esthetic experience into a political one, the questioning of art, the artwork, the artist, the spectacle, and the stage), we shall attempt to interrogate contemporary art to find out how these upheavals lead it to recast itself as well, in keeping with an alterity that helps it go beyond its 'autonomy' without lowering to the level of a service function. Techno may thus be in a position to illuminate and guide us in approaching contemporary art-forms, not, to be sure, in order to circumscribe them within a pre-established definition claiming to convey their essence, but more modestly to extract from them a series of questions enabling us to reveal tendencies, concerns, and preoccupations. That said, we hope the more prospective than synthetic nature of this work, with all the lack of precision and insufficiency that resulting from the multiplicity of fields investigated and a 'present' that will not stop happening to 'us,' will not detract from the overview we have always attempted to privilege.

Techno as a Political Laboratory of the Present
The Exhaustion of One-Way Meaning

Enchantment in a Disenchanted World

From the moment of its birth in the clubs of the United States about ten years ago and throughout its expansion, first to Europe, and then all over the world—mainly through raves—it was clear that techno was above all a festive moment. It was if the *fêtes* and partying it propagated throughout the Westernized zones of the planet brought out a desire to no longer be content with traditional or established forms of popular culture, or with the leisure and spectacle that constitute it. Yet, at least in the beginning, there was no thought of reformulating that culture or the social space through which it is transmitted and instituted. Techno displayed no interest in or claim to ideology, nor did it propose new meanings capable of renewing the configurations of contemporary community.

Unlike rock music, for example, the techno movement was not based on any political presuppositions. The absence of demand and commitment it is so often taken to task for —as if techno agreed to fade into the rules decreed by socio-economic decision-makers—does not mean it cannot be the core of a community, even a communion, however temporary and festive. If only because it has no words or text (the voice operates as pure sonority),[1] being purely instrumental or

---

[1] There are indeed few if any vocals in this music. Furthermore, when they can be heard, they are mostly present as just another instrument, valued only for their musicality, to the point

electronic, techno does not constitute a music that delivers or pro-
pounds a message. This puts it from the very start outside the political
debate within which other forms of popular music like rock, punk,
and now rap, have situated themselves.

It must then be asked whether this lack of position can be read or
explained as a renunciation, or whether it is in fact a sign quite other,
confronting us with an eminently timely process gestating new forms
of existence. Suppose the social and political fundaments and
normative ideas that have hitherto structured traditional figures of
'being-together' were in fact to reveal other possibilities for human
living, both singular and collective? Here we are not claiming that
techno in and of itself is capable of giving rise to these new forms of
existence, only that it is in effect a sign of them. What's more, techno
is without a doubt where the most concrete experimentation on a
new reconfiguration of the world is being conducted.

We shall focus our attention on how techno constitutes this
'laboratory of the present,' bearing witness' to what is happening to
our world and to the profound mutations that are redrawing its map,
requiring the individuals populating it to define new enactments of
existence.

This book takes on the challenge of showing how this movement
has had a part in changing, yet remains part of, a world and the
communicative modalities, singular and collective, that divide it, in
one and the same process of reconfiguration. We attempt to weigh the
consequences of this participation and elucidate them by basing
ourselves on what is most distinctive about techno: first of all, its
essentially festive nature, its lack of political position and commitment, relating to the exhaustion of all the great figures of 'one-way'
Meaning [*Sens unique*, in French meaning both '(only) one Meaning'

where sometimes one cannot even understand what they mean. When the voice is used, it is not,
as in other forms of Western popular music, a support for discursivity or reflexivity, but rather
for their suspension or suppression; it is not a vehicle or medium for messages at their service.
It is almost as if techno were taking as far as it will go what Deleuze and Guattari say of music,
namely that it is 'first of all a deterritorialization of the voice, which becomes less and less language.' See Gilles Deleuze et Félix Guattari, *A Thousand Plateaus*, Minneapolis, 1987.

and 'one-way (street).'—*Trans.*]—God, Reason, History, Nature—or
to what has been called 'the end of ideology.' Secondly, its relationship to contemporary technology, to machines, which derives from
the willingness, even the need, to appropriate them, then divert them,
making them from an instrument of isolation and reduction to
identity into an instrument for bringing people closer together and
for the free artistic and political expression of their singularity.

Its first principle of existence and creation is the 'mix,' a kind of
métissage, the cross-breeding of various musical sounds that corresponds to the present-day *métissage* of various cultural and ethnic
identities [as in the French and Canadian *métis* and Hispanic *mestizo*]
which, like mixing, is made possible by new technologies, or to be
more precise, in the processes of deterritorialization new technologies
have intensified to the point that the world now tends more and more
to the global.

Its stagings, neither figurative nor 'spectacular,' are in keeping
with changes and recompositions in every art-form, musical, visual,
and literary, most notably around issues of 'representation' versus
'participation,' and the questions arising from the replacement of the
former by the latter—the disappearance of the work, the disparity
between the places set aside for art and the fluid, ephemeral nature of
their coming-into-being, the role of the artist, and the place of the
spectator, among others. But whether or not techno is responding to
this profound transformation of the world, or whether that makes it
not just, or no longer, a mere extension of traditional popular culture,
but rather an original and unprecedented form of being-in-the-world
and being-in-the-body, does not mean it deliberately constitutes itself
in response to these mutations, as if emanating from some avant-garde
or revolutionary will to make history. It does in fact respond, or rather
correspond, to a historical logic where is is not so much techno that
makes contemporary history as the latter that produces and calls it
forth, reveals it, and sets it in motion.

We may thus be tempted to venture than nothing is in a better position than raves to bear witness to what is happening in and to our time,

our community, which now has to invent itself out of the collapse of the myths and ideologies that previously warranted coherence and permanence, and out of the technological development of a world whose boundaries are less and less marked or secured. Yet, without claiming any ideology or proposing any meaning or a new myth on which to stage a rally, techno nonetheless creates bonds of intimacy among the individuals who participate. But by doing so above and beyond existing accords and contracts, all the traditional forms of the 'theologico-political,' it may seem as if were bound for nothing. But there is no need to resemble, either by race or blood, in political or religious allegiance, in order to reassemble. This is the truth of techno and the festive it revives, opening up a space for sharing no longer based exclusively on the needs of the socio-economic and political order. In this regard, it presents itself as a return—if only an ephemeral one, since its time is the time of the festive—to a sharing and communication that no longer entail the separation and isolation of individuals. To the contrary, it grounds itself in a common existence; only there can they fully, completely exist, thus responding to the fundamental demands of their being.

The festive is born, so to speak, of the sacrifice of order and utility. It exists solely in order to exceed them, to remove the common ground on which they base themselves and organize their existence. What it gives rise to in its place is a relationship where single beings no longer need truth or authority of any kind in order to understand each other and be together. This also implies that an existence hemmed in by the limits of the social and the imperatives of daily life (work, consumption) would be devoid of all meaning or fulfilment if it were not able to temporarily exceed those limits, particularly through festive practices. Therein lies the polarizing and contagious power of techno, and this is what makes it so popular today, giving it the same capacity the festive has, indeed is, for intensively sharing existence. In this sense, when we are engaged or involved in it, we touch each other with nothing, and it may even be because we have 'nothing,' no meaning, no message to communicate or send, that we are able to touch each other. And all the more so, since, in this age deserted by the shades of old, whether divine or metaphysical, it alone seems capable of of opening up a communicative space to satisfy that imperious and unstoppable human demand for sharing and communion—at least of emotions—so constitutive of existence. As a result, each festivity, today each rave, replays the the relating and sharing while preventing it from being reified or petrified into something contractual or dissolving into a religious or political communion.

Being thus a resistance to anything that closes off the political, or that attempts a closure of being-together in its totality, the festive suggests, or perhaps may always have admitted, that there is nothing that can appropriate or take over the sharing, which it always overflows or exceeds. Indeed, this overflow is the only way to understand the agitation manifest and resonating in techno, the sight and sound of our world fracturing and trying to recompose itself in another form, in accordance with a set of relations no longer reposing on Idols or Ideals. Indeed, 'it all seems to happen as if the effervescence which controls the interior life of groups, the permanent revolution which endlessly modifies social structures and attempts to set up new ones. . . were concentrated in ecstatic ceremonies' whose present-day form is raves.[2]

This means that in sum the the festive bears witness to the mutations and transformations which have, either visibly or underground, upset the inertia of traditions, religions, and political systems that has enabled them to enfold themselves immutably cloistered in their identity. Should we not then see in the apolitical stance of this movement something other than blithe resignation or a renunciation of any willingness to change society? The apolitical may in this sense constitute an essential stratum, constitutive in turn of the social and the political. All things considered, far from being an 'archaic,' 'primitive,' 'irresponsible,' or 'dangerous' individual and collective behavior, as one sometimes reads, as if ravers were all marginal types incapable of meeting the demands and goals of our society, the techno movement poses, or rather recalls, the demand for another relationship of humanity to itself, and particularly to its body. Whatever one thinks of it, it constitutes a contemporary figuration (or configuration) of

[2] Jean Duvignaud, *Le Don du rien*, Paris, 1977

'expenditure,' festive and transgressive practices, and more precisely in this respect, practices of the body. It is certainly no coincidence this new figuration of being-in-the-world and being-in-the-body has arisen through an apolitical musical movement whose rhythms set the body in action, even putting the dancing body into a trance. Thus, as Jean-Luc Nancy put it in *Corpus*, 'Our world happens to have deployed a rhythmic world-ness, one of jazz and rap and beyond, a press, profusion and congestion, a popular-ness of posture and position, with a electronic skin, zoned and massed (and massaged), of *noise*, one could even say, for there is indeed a background noise that grows when forms have neither soundness nor sense (social, common, sentimental, or metaphysical). Yes, noise: it's something like the verso, the underside of a thought, but also the rumble within the folds of the body.'[3]

This makes techno something more than a fashion phenomenon supposed to disappear as quickly as it appeared. This deserves our attention, for in becoming ever more marginalized, practices of expenditure and festivity themselves have difficulty resisting their subordination to the empire of thing and number. Also, when the festive becomes a thing to be consumed, its meaning, too, tends to be erased and disappear, engulfing with it nothing less that the totality of existence. Does this imply that existence is humanly possible only within the horizon-line of the festive? Definitely not.[4] It's just that it begins only in laughter and shared feeling, with the sharing of non-goal-oriented practices, those not systematically governed only by the imperatives of work and rational accumulation. Unlike the productive working rhythms than mark time in the lives both of men and efficient machines, techno, and the festiveness in it, has not been subordinated

---

[3] Jean-Luc Nancy, *Corpus*, Paris, 1992.

[4] As Georges Bataille demonstrated, 'The endless problem posed by the impossibility of being human without being a thing, and of going beyond the limits of a thing without returning to animal slumber finds a limited solution in the fête, the festive.' In Theory of Religion, New York, 1992. For Bataille the fête is, along with eroticism, one of the privileged figures of 'expenditure,' through which man escapes the circle of utilitarian activities which inevitably drag him into a process of reification.

to any outside goal or usefulness. It may indeed mean the suspension of those goals, momentarily interrupting the teleological logic humans assume in their productive activities.

The central meaning of techno is that human life cannot be wholly reduced to utility and servility, and it invites participants to sever the bonds of a life fettered to itself, with no other goal but optimal comfort. Because its festiveness provides in some fashion a space for the expenditure and transgression of our Western modernity, they may also also draw man back to his ancestral practices and customs, opening up a space to resonate with the echo of the bacchanalia and orgiastic delirium that have populated the margins of our history. Raves, which can be considered the Dionysia of modern times, may in this sense be as old as man himself. We should not forget that humans, alongside the laws and norms they have created and continue to create for themselves in order to construct their singular and collective existence, have always set aside, during festive periods, moments of transgression during which they exceed and upset the imperious order of clear and organizing consciousness, replacing it with the disorder of a deluge of the senses and common feeling.

Even if they no longer truly partake of the religious or sacred, raves bear witness to a resistance or recurrence of festiveness and 'expenditure,' as if man had always felt a need to discover and share zones of excess. Techno provides a opening for that expenditure and for the sacred, one that might seem in contradiction with its lack of political or religious commitment, although here the sacred has become something purely formal and remains only a shell. It proves, by providing an actual experience of it, that the sacred may vanish from social space without taking with it the demand for surpassing or exceeding oneself it necessarily involves. Here, too, as it was for Durkheim, the festive is the means through which society produces sacredness, and when it is envisioned and experienced within the horizon-line of techno, it expels or exhausts all mythological and socio-historical determinations, as if in the end only the *fête*, as sharing of non- and 'an-'economic existence, can henceforth be sacred. One can easily see that techno, despite bearing the the earmark of our time—the exhaustion of political and religious forms—techno nonetheless bases itself on an appeal to communion, but a paradoxical one effected around a hollow or 'empty' kernel. Indeed, the communing, though grounded in shared, chorus-like enthusiasm, preserves of its meaning, or need for meaning, only the formal shell or envelope, as if the third term of the relationship were were, so to speak, 'empty' or 'hollow,' leaving only the simple fact of being together, in common, totally involved in the same event. Here the being-together exists only in the actuality of the dancing bodies, and is not based on any community of fact or appearance except the *fête* being shared at that moment. Techno adopts only the outward form of possession or mystical communion, as if it were in some sense a secularized and desacralized figure of it, where it is revealed to man that the sacred is not god, gods, or spirits who 'mount' or 'surmount' him, but the trance itself, the momentary but shared vanishing of consciousness into the moment. In other words, this makes the transcendent, in its many geo- and historico-political guises, into a pretext for the limited return to the pure immanence in which the world of consciousness dissolves into the present.

Yet this festive aspect, as Bataille clearly showed, is not necessarily fulfilled (except at the risk of leading to the 'worst catastrophes') in some reconstitution of an individual or collective 'sovereignty,' but only demonstrates the polymorphous and ineradicable need, at work in every culture and at all latitudes, to leave behind the world as reflected and ordered by consciousness and sink momentarily over the horizon and into the dark night of the moment.

But there is no access to the moment except in the suspension or vanishment, itself limited, of the continuity of time, which underlies and structures the contractual social and rational order. This is certainly what is in play in the festivities of techno, to wit, the possibility, with no prior knowledge or teleology, neither watchword nor commandment, of self-abandon in the present, and of a sharing of that abandon as if it were the greatest gift. As soon as the moment becomes an opening up of existence to its aneconomic dimension, we can easily understand why our capitalist societies refuse, by their very essence, the possibility of self-abandon, obliging us to center—and decenter ourselves—on the project. Indeed, within the horizons of economic individualism—our individualism—the projecting, calculation, and forecasting of what is to come constitute the temporal modalities of being-in-the-world. Existence never abandons itself to itself, to its presence in the moment. It is always a tending towards, projecting. Man as such constructs his own humanity, but in opting for one lone and pure project, he renounces it, accepting the opaque visage of machine and number. Only the project has value, which, because it is 'the postponement of existence until later,'[5] means that existence has meaning only to the extent we renounce it. It is easy to see the principle of Christianity here, of which, in this regard, capitalism is a present-day secularized figure. Techno can, of course, only express its opposition to the fact that existence is ordained exclusively on this sacrifice of the present with a view to the future. As we shall see below, it uses technics, not for the future, but for the moment, the time of existence, literally *ek-sist-entia*, 'standing outside or beside oneself,' ecstasy. If that goes back to other forms of music, like rock, for example, with techno one cannot help being struck by the primacy of the demand for a shared present, as if beyond and in it it were a whole epoch, ours, expressing an imperative not to give in to the future, some 'radiant future,' rather to be somehow caught up by and in the present, lived or experienced collectively. Here we can only refer generally to the work of Michel Maffesoli, and to the interview he has accorded us in the present volume. As is clear from his own analysis of various social phenomena, none of the many contemporary political and esthetic forms can be comprehended without what he calls an 'ethics of' or 'concern for the present' that distinguishes our time from modernity and its project, with its mode of being wholly tended towards the future, and in the name of which existence itself is to be sacrificed.[6] It is

[5] Georges Bataille, *The Inner Experience*, New York, 1988.
[6] Michel Maffesoli, *The Shadow of Dionysos: A Contribution to the Sociology of the Orgy*, New York, 1993.

in 'the hollow left by the absence of project in its various forms that another manner of understanding and living life in society can find a niche.'[7]

Here we are confronted with a kind of intensification of the energy invested in daily life, all the greater since it is no longer tended toward attaining a goal or realizing some end. This does not mean, however, there is a generalized lack of interest in the future, but perhaps only that the future can no longer determine either the ordination or the subordination of our singular and collective existences as a whole. It is as if, in the midst of the exhaustion of all the ideologies and utopias of 'progress' and the concomitant multiplication of lesser and more ephemeral collective events, there was some resurgence of a communitarian wisdom of the shared moment, revealing the need to be-together around some 'nothing' (nothing ideological or religious, in any case). This means, then, that collective existence is not exhausted or depleted in the collapse of its projects and political figures, but infinitely exceeds or overruns the logic of its figuration or self-appropriation through the mediation of a 'full' or 'unique' kernel of meaning, whether mythological or ideological. In other words, what is finished or exhausted is not the collective, as we are endlessly told, but only its Western logic, namely the project of making the community into a work, an artwork to be executed according to some meaning, either given (divine transparence) or produced (the transparence of Reason or Progress).

The opening up of an existence which no longer recognizes truth anywhere but in the present, thus rendering obsolete all the 'hinterworlds,' or other utopian worlds, that have until now governed and determined our collective behaviors, channeling them paroxysmally into the worst totalitarian catastrophes, Communist and Fascist, of the twentieth century. Or could it be that, conversely, it is the exhaustion of an Ideal to be attained which has now cleared some common time and space, where, in common, existence can be lived and shared in the present.

[7] Michel Maffesoli, *Au creux des apparences : pour une éthique de l'esthétique*, Paris, 1993.

In either case, the demand for the present as an exhaustion of the ideological or utopian requires us (or invites, as the poet Friedrich Hölderlin had it long ago) to 'turn the desire to leave this world for the other into a desire to leave some other world for this one.'[8]

There is indeed nothing further to produce, project or re-enact, which goes along with the interruption of the West as a search and demand for meaning. The fact that there is nothing more, nor a way out of the finitude of meaning, opens up existence to another space of sharing within which it is no longer possible to decently, if that is the word, await the return or coming of any god or other new myth. 'And if the absence were a sign, telling us that we should no longer dream of ways out but stand fast on this site, supposedly with no exit, and become familiar with it, rather than chase after the usual 'ways out.'[9] This is the question of our time, and it demands of us new ways of conducting our existences in common, in that double movement evoked earlier, of being open to the present and withdrawing from any enchanting future.

To the extent, then, that it incarnates or incorporates into itself the collapse of the great communitarian foundations, reposing only on a communion through music and dance, techno is akin to a kind of enchantment in a disenchanted world, an enchantment that in some sense is nothing more than experience shared in, through, and as the disappearance of all watchwords or ideologies. In some sense it's as if these foundations were losing their cohesive force, bringing about the disappearance of traditional social and political segmentations or partitions, and giving rise in the wake of their very exhaustion to the coming of a 'world-ness' (if only a 'rhythmic' one), a worldness of bodies and being-in-the-body revealed in the rhythm of techno music. 'The systolic rhythm of techno revives the perspective of a historic mutation, or at least its vanishing point: its sought-after hypnotic effect fits in well with the new forms of rejecting and subverting the values of our society. Obsessive repetition as against sweetening through melody,

[8] In Friedrich Hölderlin, *Œuvres*, Paris, 1967.
[9] Martin Heidegger, *Basic Concepts,* Bloomington, 1993.

hysterical muteness as against chatter; the importance accorded the
voice as against the loss of meaning of words; the transmigrations of
young people towards the the sites of our post-industrial society,
abandoned factories, hangars and warehouses, as against the disen-
chantment of industrial society and the loss of public space.'[10]

Without in any way making it its theme or message, techno, in its
loud silence, implies that the old socio-historic figures of meaning no
longer make sense, and consequently can no longer fragment or
partition the world according to an ethnic or political score that until
now has divided it up into separate and opposed identities. The new
music, eminently cosmopolitan, will be that of the commons of the
world.

The Alliance of Dionysus and Prometheus

What is new is that the festive, which is and remains the only
watchword of techno, be articulated through technics and made
possible through machines, for in general the festive opens a space for
man where there is no room for machines. One could retort that this is
not so new, since radios and televisions have long been machines to
relax and instruct man and gladden his existence. But is listening to the
radio or watching television still a festive practice, or is it an activity
that belongs more to leisure and spectacle, in the end a parody or
simulacrum of the festive?

The point is not to replace leisure and spectacle with the festive, as if the
former served no justifiable need. It's just that when they absorb the whole
of festive practice and claim to somehow stand in its stead, or to constitute
the modern and secularized figure of the festive, as if the latter were some
outmoded or 'primitive' image of the human species, it is humanity itself
which is mutilated, in its integrity and entirety. Furthermore, one could say
it is not the machine that alienates man, isolating him by reducing human
existence to stereotyped behaviors. Machines are neutral and have no value

[10] Béatrice Durupt, in *Digraphe* n°68

other than those we inject them with. It is time we realize, as Félix Guattari proposed, that 'we can judge such a machinic evolution neither positively nor negatively,' for technics is not the diabolical being we too easily make it out to be. Nor is it, inversely, as we may have thought at one point in modernity, an automatic motor of ethical progress. In fact, 'it all depends on its articulation with the collective workings of utterance.'[11] It is up to us, if we wish to be more than mere spectators of our own destiny, to take an active part in this 'articulation.' What in fact alienates humans, in providing for expenditure only in leisure and spectacle, is a system in which machines function and functionalize human life—that is, capitalism, or rather the ultra-free-market capitalism now becoming the only 'collective workings of utterance,' to the point where it can seem puerile and naive to question it or propose some alternative.

As a consequence, there is no longer any room for aneconomic activity. As Jean Duvignaud puts it, 'Our societies have channeled giving. They have encased it in exchange-value and economic procedure' in such a way that 'we are born into and die in a world without the festive, or rather a world of festivities carefully controlled by regulating ideologies insuring the cohesiveness of capitalist and socialist societies.'[12]

Thus, modern capitalist societies (and even Communism, which according to Marx was to be fully realized only in its third stage, that of a 'society of leisure') exclude in principle the festiveness of collective practices, not only because it is judged to be useless, but mainly because it seems a potential danger, a contagious threat of disorder which, like a flame fed by the wind, disturbs social order. Indeed, all state power tends by its very nature and essence to eliminate festive practices, for the latter can only exist by transgressing the limits and prohibitions that structure and define them.

This is the reason why it is important to replace them with leisure and spectacle, for in the latter, participants can have fun without ceasing to consume or overstepping the bounds that keep them isolated or closed up within themselves. Thus, 'the media exhort us to celebrate

[11] Félix Guattari, *Chaosmosis: An Ethicoæsthetic Paradigm,* Bloomington, 1995.
[12] Ibid.

the significant moments of our lives in this pseudo-unification of commodity and spectacle, this famous non-event of pure representation. In response to this obscenity, we can avail ourselves, on one hand, of a range of refusals (as illustrated by the Situationists) and, on the other, of the emergence of a culture of the festive, aloof from and unknown to the self-proclaimed organizers of our leisure.'[13]

It is above all because they are a living and present form of the festive, the revival of the Dionysiac in a West coming to its end, that raves are now being demonized. Everything is being done to suppress them, either by simply banning them or by moving them into clubs or discothèques, even into halls intended for traditional spectacles, thus neutralizing them. This is a devious way of controlling, even anesthetizing them—authorizing them as they are integrated into an economic circuit where they can only be gradually transformed and reified into spectacle and leisure. This is without a doubt where the greatest threat to the techno movement lies, where it risks losing its soul, so to speak, becoming another spectacle just like the others, something we are already seeing. The worst thing is not being banned, but being turned into spectacle.[14]

This is how something that starts out free and alive, evolving on the edge of a society to which it brings otherness, is always absorbed by that society and reified into commodity, specifically into commodity spectacle. The Situationists showed how spectacles become part of a general economy of representation within which they function like a product meant to be consumed and from which the maximum profit is to be derived. Through its recognition, institutionalization, and integration into traditional festive spaces, techno is becoming commodified by applying to it the same recipes used in rock concerts: a greater centrality or frontality of the stage, a star system or specta-

[13] Hakim Bey, *T. A. Z, The Temporary Autonomous Zone Ontological Anarchy, Poetic Terrorism,* New York, 1991.
[14] For the last year, at least in France, there has been a noticeable change on the part of the authorities with regard to techno. They have gone from outright rejection to the beginnings of a dialogue that can only be encouraged, even if here we once again see the specter of a commodification of the spectacle rearing its head.

cularity applied to DJs, time limitations, high prices, and so on. The absorption, appropriation and promotion by society of that which tries to escape it, as is the case today with raves, does not unfailingly imply that there is no resistance on the part of the festive. On the contrary, it attempts to reconstitute itself even as it is being co-opted. What's more, the proliferation of small record labels in the music industry, like the continuation of organized festivities outside the official circuit (in what are called 'free parties' or teknivals), prove that the field has not been wholly contaminated or neutralized.[15]

In consequence, even if the success of raves can be explained principally by the fact that they have revived and reactivated bonding and sharing power from a state of exhaustion, even with rock, it behooves us to nuance our critique somewhat (as both Jean-Luc Nancy and Michel Maffesoli do in the interviews in the present volume), if only because with the spectacle, as with the commercial, there is always the possibility of something being recreated around the edges; this is equally true of the commercial spectacle. One cannot deny the pleasures and shared feelings to be found there.

It may thus seem surprising, even contradictory, that the techno movement has been attracted to machines and technology, generally considered a power for separating and isolating individuals, a power for enslaving and shackling bodies. But it is precisely because of their potential to favor the free development of sociability and 'world-ness,' as well as of the body, that they have been claimed and promoted for techno, as if, far from separating singular existences, they might in fact contribute to commingling them more than political ideals could. It is not the least of the paradoxes surrounding techno that it is through the technological that the tendency to transgression—to phenomena of trance and ecstasy—survives and revives. It was this tendency the

[15] This also relates to another aspect of techno, its self-production and management. What has until now made this festivity so remarkable is that most of the time they are organized in places not intended for such events. Similarly, the music has been produced and distributed by small independent record labels that the major record companies are now trying to take over. Unlike the rock music, or even rap, of today, techno is a culture that has developed on the edges of society, even though this is less obvious now that it has grown so much.

Western world had rejected as it came into being in ancient Greece, which attempted to eradicate or contain it through technics. So it is through what had distanced it from Dionysiac violence that the latter reappears. Raves show there is a certain irony at work in the resurgence of the aspiration to an ecstatic collective and singular existence from within new musical technologies, when technics has always been mobilized to tame, even exclude, the excesses of Dionysus.[16] Raves thereby demonstrate for our own time that a life enslaved only to the demands of work and technics is inevitably impoverished if it cannot at some moment abandon itself to the festive or to expenditure. But nor is there reason to reject them outright, for technology in its multiple forms has the potential to favor the free development of existence in common and rapport between individuals.

Furthermore, we are given the impression, often without any clear explanation, that technics is a kind of substance or essence developing by itself through history, as if there were in the multiplicity of particulars a unity that combined them all, delineating some autonomous process independent of human control, one we will not be able to control any better than nature itself. It is easy to see how such a reading can legitimate or justify all kinds of reactionary and conservative thinking, as well as all kinds of naive utopias of a return to nature or to the authenticity of an existence free of machines. This is nothing new; it is easy to imagine that the fear of technics is as old as technics itself. Remember the astronomers of the Vatican who refused even to look into Galileo's telescope. What frightens humanity is precisely its capacity to transform the world in which we live, for those transformations can in turn elude its control and close in on it again like another nature. As vain and sterile as it might be, this fear at least has the merit of laying bare what constitutes the essence of technics,

---

[16] From this we may deduce that 'in a sense there is synergy, at least symbolically, between technology and the desire for something else, for trance, to be able to step outside oneself, or for an enchanted world,' so that in our own time, 'post-modernity' may be defined as 'the synergy between archaic elements and technological development.' Michel Maffesoli, *Des effervescences festives*, interview with Michel Gaillot, in Blocnotes, n°13, October 1996.

namely 'the "essential technicity" of existence as a non-essence and a surrogation of being.'[17]

In other words technics is proper to man to the extent that he is without essence. Unlike any other existent, man is not, nor does he become, automatically—instinctually—himself; he has to make himself into man. In this sense, technics, far from being a gigantic Satanic machine that enslaves our existence, is the means through which man becomes a work of his own, and which allows him to self-constitute and exist as man. It designates the set of prostheses through which human beings further their existence. What appears so frightening about technics is nothing more than the angst man feels before, and in, the exposure of his existence to the abyss of his lack of essence. Furthermore, since technics is what is proper to us, our nature, it cannot simply be discarded or rejected. The question is how to appropriate it for ourselves, to take possession of it. For when it eludes us, escapes our mastery, it is, so to speak, our own intimacy and freedom which also steal away. We can understand, then, why the techno movement has claimed our attention, for in its will to appropriation of technics, to not simply leave it to the specialists and rescue it from its purely utilitarian and economic uses, it is breaking new ground for humanity. It in no way claims to have accomplished this task, or any other task, for that matter. Because it has no other end than the festive—to create and spend—it reveals to us that existence, or what is most inalienable about it, its freedom, can draw on technics as a means of flourishing, and even more, a means of sharing that flourishing. In sum, if 'Prometheus needs Dionysus,' as Maffesoli says, we should also recognize that Dionysus needs Prometheus. The originality of techno lies in the fact that it articulates or reconciles expenditure and technics, or more precisely, puts one at the service of the other, effecting an opening for an existence made whole again within the 'machinic' world. What is techno if not ecstatic sharing made possible by machines?

[17] Jean-Luc Nancy, *Une Pensée finie*, Paris, 1990.

In our world, and in an existence more and more permeated with technology, techno bears witness to the fact that machines do not prevent man from being himself; on the contrary, they are how he comes to exist, or more precisely, the by and in which he exists today. In the end, we must understand that 'he who refuses the final consequences of technics must also refuse the very first signs of it; but then it is man itself, in his freedom and coming-to-be, in his relationship to himself, that he will ultimately be refusing.'[18] But what is most remarkable is how with cyberspace (CD-ROMs, digital video, and the Internet, for example) to which it is also related, techno takes over technics and appropriates it for non-technical and non-economic ends. Beginning with, and within, the horizons of contemporary technology, it inaugurates new forms of sensibility and thought, of esthetic creation and interpretation. Already the esthetic originality of this music—that which is proper to it—could not have developed without the machines invented by contemporary technics. It is based on a principle of composition and performance which consists of 'making music with music,' as DJ Derrick May put it. In this sense, techno does not appear to be original creation, but rather a reappropriation and reconfiguration of various forms of already existing sounds, which it then joins, and mixes, transfiguring them into a new composition. This reappropriation and reconfiguration of the old, of pre-existing sound material, only found the right conditions for its existence with the appearance of new technologies (samplers, sequencers, synthesizers, and so on) that no longer require special training or technical skills to make music. Besides the fact that they allow one to put together an infinity of different musical forms, these machines, especially the sampler, shift the field of experimentation and creation from composition based on notes to one effected through recordings. The sampler, which is a computer that can appropriate and transform any sound, is in one sense a completely new instrument, one that can only extend the domain of

[18] Maurice Blanchot, *Friendship*, Palo Alto, 1997.

musical creativity, but which which also changes its form and requirements.[19]

Although it was really created little more than ten years ago,
techno has become the most vernacular figure of electronic music. It
goes back to the earlier work of Pierre Schaeffer and Pierre Henry,
Terry Riley and Steve Reich, John Cage, but also to Kraftwerk. It is
important to emphasize that unlike earlier electronic music, it is a
music for dancing, a festive music intended not only for the mind,
but, on the contrary, to engage existence in its totality (body and soul,
one might say). Thus, although technics incontestably constitutes
conditions for the possibility of techno, the latter only acquires it
special coloration, its affective and emotional tonality, by appealing to
another dimension, that of the body and its enthusiasms, as when it is
engaged in dance. 'Technica' and Africa, one might say, are the two
essential poles of techno. It is no coincidence that this music was first
invented and played by American blacks, who breathed into it its
more somatic and festive side.

But we do not have on one side work, reason, and technics, deter-
mining what is possible with machines, and, on the other, *fête*, sensibility, and the emotions—'natural,' 'authentic' existence, pure and free
of any artifice. If only with its own machines, techno suspends this
dichotomy, proving that art, *fête*, and technology are not necessarily

[19] This whole argument about esthetics and 'creation' assuredly deserves greater development
and detail than the present context can provide, given the constraints within which a book such
as this one is produced. For more, we refer the reader to the proceedings of a colloquium at the
art-space *Confort Moderne* in Poitiers, France, to the articles by Jean-Yves Loup in the revues
Blocnotes and Crash, and, even though it concerns itself more with rap than with techno, to
Richard Shusterman, *Pragmatic Æsthetics: Living Beauty, Rethinking Art*, Blackwell, 1992. The
latter is instructive, especially concerning the changes brought about by sampling, the creation
of the new out of the old, mixing, and 'the challenge issued to the traditional ideal of originality and uniqueness' in art, bearing witness to the esthetic mutations concerning contemporary
art, the artwork, and the artist. From here we easily move on to the question of 'post-modernism,' that epoch characterized particularly by 'a tendency to recycling and appropriation of
someone else's materials rather than originality; the eclectic mixing of styles; enthusiastic loyal-
ty to new technology and mass culture; challenging modern notions of esthetic autonomy and
artistic purity; an accent on temporal and spatial localization rather than on the universal and
eternal.'

and irremediably irreconcilable and incompatible. For this reason, and many others, it is no longer possible to belive that human existence and technics are separated by impermeable and intangible boundaries demarcating two antagonistic universes. Consequently, instead of seeing in the new technologies a simple continuation or consolidation of technics within human existence we can only passively accept, it seems to us, on the contrary, that we have been given a chance to reconquer and strengthen our freedom and autonomy in relation to all other political, technical and economic power. This is why our appropriation of these machines, in a world that is tending more and more towards globality, no doubt constitutes the most responsible attitude we can take. It is in this sense that the techno movement seems to us so exemplary, as if the demand for participation, to no longer be a mere spectator, were now driving the process of figuration and transformation of the world by these new technologies.

However, the contribution of machines to these festive and esthetic ends is itself only possible because technics and machines have themselves changed and are no longer the same. It is certainly no coincidence that techno developed in Detroit, in 1987 (and house a year earlier in Chicago), just at a time and place when a certain level of technics and equipment was reaching its end or a point of exhaustion, dragging down with it the world they had given rise to, and another era was beginning with the introduction of personal computers into many American homes. One only has to think of that city, one of the technological marvels of America, and now devastated by the collapse of the industrial world. Techno is in one sense an index of this change or mutation, itself possible only because contemporary technics is now deployed in new forms no longer solely based in the mechanical, but also, and especially, in the electronic and digital.

Just like the mechanical age of technics that preceded it, the electronic age will also open up a new world, modifying and recomposing it in its totality. This is also how 'burdensome machines, requiring great collective efforts to function, generally become a tool of repression wielded by the state. Bells. Galleys. Cannons. Tanks. But tools that can be owned and used on an individual scale inevitably bring with them democratic revolutions.'[20] In its mechanical and industrial form, technics was at the origin of the machines that replaced the physical energy of man, and of the animals he made use of, whereas in its present form, it installs a set of electronic machines that extend or enlarge the human brain and nervous system to the world in its globality. The primary benefit of these new technologies is that each of us is now in a position to appropriate and control them, so that henceforth machines, and technics in general, will no longer belong exclusively to the political and economic powers that be, and no longer depend on their authority and decisions. All such revolutions, it may be noted, have afforded people greater autonomy by allowing them to emancipate themselves, first from their material conditions of existence, and then from religious and political decision-making centers.

With the appearance of new technologies, in particular those having to do with communications, man and machine are no longer in conflict. As a consequence, the image of man being alienated by the machine disappears in favor of a much more positive one, that of a possible emancipation of existence, and of one's autonomy, through electronic communication. One only has to think of the Internet or the Web, for example. Because the stakes are so high and the implications so great—human freedom itself is in play—'info-poverty' is one of the major problems of our time. But in fact this has always been the case. But since today everything develops in accelerated fashion, to the point where the world is exposed to it in its globality, the problem calls for, even requires, a particular attention and responsibility, since it is all of humanity now being cast and put into play. But so as not to fall into a naive and hypocritical utopianism, we must not forget that although there is no emancipatory effect except through technology, the latter is real and effective only when it is shared and democratized; it can no longer remain a matter only for specialists or technicians. Since it is what makes man man, technics needs to be shared; those

---

[20] Timothy Leary, quoted *ibid.*

who would attempt to monopolize on it would thereby lay claim to a monopoly on humanity, depriving everyone else of it. Here we are concerned with the right to be oneself, by oneself, with the right to be an actor of one's own humanity. In this regard the interaction and interactivity between man and machine creates the possibility of no longer remaining a spectator, a receiver of information. This is all the more important now that, since McLuhan, we know how much those who select and control information determine the figuration of the world and of our existence, as well as of the event-horizon in which we take root and open ourselves to alterity. This underscores that we must not leave this control to political or economic powers, in other words that we need to transform vertical structures for transmitting informatiom into a horizontal network where each of us is equal before communication. Cyberspace offers man individual machines thanks to which he need no longer remain passive, and can become an actor in his own formation and information. On the world-scale of such mutations, which offer us the chance for a 'cosmopolitic' world (if we learn how to seize it) it is now time for us to accept that what we find so frightening about technics and machines comes only from our lack of being or essence, that is, from our finitude (whose particular technics is the prosthesis). It is further time to recognize in it the meaning we have always strived to find in some divine or spiritual figure. The rejection of the machine on the pretext that it is an instrument or weapon of capitalism is a puerile and dangerous behavior, tantamount to 'giving someone a stick to beat you with.'[21] Let us on the contrary take hold of it, benefiting from the possibility being offered to us of appropriating the machine in order to recover our autonomy, diverting it to festive and artistic ends. Appropriating and diverting, through and of technology—these are the watchwords of techno, the means through which it makes itself into a popular culture

---

[21] This is no doubt the best way to look at technics if we see it as something that closes in around our existences, like some imprisoning or enslaving power. It is then, as Deleuze and Guattari suggest, that 'the high-end technology for enslavement of the world-system is invoked. But even, or especially, this "machinic" enslavement is rife in undecidable motion and proposition. Far from requiring the knowledge of a sworn specialist, they provide weapons for becoming to everybody in the whole world.' Deleuze and Guattari, *A Thousand Plateaus.*

of a technical kind, and, as we declared at the outset, through which it becomes a artistic and political laboratory of the present. We would be wrong to see in it only a marginal and insignificant consequence of technological development, for its constitutive principle makes it into nothing less than a total experience of existence in the conditions of life on earth in their present, and clearing new paths for the world of tomorrow (although that is not its specific goal here). It acts from an intuition that what is operative politically and esthetically in the present, especially with respect to the creation of singular and collective bodies, now lies essentially in the development of technics, no longer in ideological struggle.

Horizontalizing the World

Furthermore, it is neither accidental nor anodyne that the mixing and *métissage* of various musical forms and identities occurring in techno consists of echoes, on an esthetic level, the political *métissage* of ethnic and national identities, also entailed by or originating in technics, in the form of a technological coming-to-be of the world (or the coming-to-be-world of technology, tantamount to the same thing)[22]. In techno, the mixing of identities or different musical genres (jazz, rock, disco, pop, reggae, rap, and classical music) is not only tolerated or accepted, but central; indeed, it defines the very foundation and principles of this music and its esthetics. Nor is it a coincidence that it has come to be a transcultural or transnational, even 'world,' form of popular music (in any case the most global form that has ever been invented).

It is hard to overstate how striking and significant the comparison between mixing, the creative principle of techno, and *métissage*, the process of opening up national and ethnic identities implied by the development of new communicative technologies actually is. Technics is in one sense a condition for the possibility of the

---

[22] This argument concerning the relation of mixing to *métissage* is developed at greater length and in more detail in my article '*Du mix au métissage. La techno comme désacralisation du monde*,' published in an issue devoted to machines of the journal *L'Animal*, n°4, November 1997.

métissage of musical forms and identities by which techno is defined, just as it is for ethnic and national ones which are redrawing the map of the world. It is by its very essence 'trans-ethnic,' as Bernard Stiegler has shown in his analysis of the work of Leroi-Gourhan. That is, it develops via 'networks' (of communications) throughout multiple human communities. As a consequence, and as part of the same process whereby it links and opens up those ethnic identities to each other, it is a simultaneous 'conquest and loss of territory,' and thus also swept along in 'an irresistible process of deterritorialization.' This process, set in motion by what he calls 'ethno-technic coming-into-being,' results, however, in 'a suspension of the ethnic differences themselves, at least of those differences that remain traditional, by which is meant rooted in a territory,' which gives rise to 'a confusion or melting of the ethnos into a mega-ethnos.'[23]

The mutations occurring in the present, which originated in the passage from a mechanical technics to electronic technology, accelerate and amplify this process of deterritorialization, the uprooting of the ethnos from the territory through which it defines itself. Thus, 'with the new technologies, to the extent that they provide cultural models which are not, at least initially, rooted in the local context but are formed with a view to diffusion over the surface of the globe, we have a remarkable means of overcoming the obstacles set up by traditional cultures to the seizure, transit, and communication of information.' In other words, 'the new technologies are in the process of removing the hurdles presented by human life an earth.'[24] By multiplying communications networks over the face of the planet, these technologies, for the first time, give people in all their ethnic and geopolitical diversity, the possibility of pooling their memory in common and sharing, in electronic form, a common language or idiom. We are at the dawn of a new cosmology, about to enter what might be called 'techno-cosmology,' where the map of the world, its

---

[23] Bernard Stiegler, *La Programmatologie de Leroi-Gourhan*, in *Les Nouvelles de l'Archéologie*, n°48-49,1992.
[24] Jean-François Lyotard, *The Inhuman: Reflections on Time*, Palo Alto, 1992.

limits and borders, must all be redrawn, along with our ways of being together and sharing.

As technics becomes world, we realize that 'dwelling' in technics or 'welcoming' it, is nothing more than dwelling in and welcoming the finitude of meaning.[25] In the end, nothing but technics can come as surrogate to our lack of being. Instead of reinforcing the confinement and enclosure of identity, it pushes identities to open up and experience alterity increasingly by crossing the borders that have kept them enfolded within themselves. By accelerating to the level of globality, the forces of deterritorialization now put into play work toward the secularization of the collective in all its forms. From now on, these will tend more and more to slip *through* territories, 'crossing' them rather than putting down roots, as if in the end the deterritorialization that technics implies were but the other side of *métissage*. One can easily understand why all nationalisms (like the National Fronts in various countries), all extremisms based on identity, are so radically opposed to such 'cross-breeding' and globalization. Their very survival is indeed at stake. We can also understand why our era has become the theater for a multiplicity of lesser communitarian forms resembling those we find in techno.

We are now embarking on a new age where this being-together will be played out, created and invented in a different fashion, according to a polarity determined not by belonging, but by elective choice. Indeed, if human relations or communications are no longer, or decreasingly, based on a received meaning heir, either by roots or belonging, to an identity or a territory, there remains only 'electiveness' as a modality for sharing non- or a-territorial, that is, trans-ethnic or trans-national community.

The multiplication of communications networks throughout the world by the new technologies opens up, on the collective level, a horizon of new possibilities, other possibilities, within which alliances are being woven beyond the level of communities of fact and

[25] Jean-Luc Nancy, *Une Pensée finie*.

obligation. This leads to what might be called 'elective communities,' and implies that forms of being-together define their relations as elective singularities (according to taste, shared feeling, or friendship). This makes for the most open and free communities possible, non-prescriptive and non-coerced, where ethnic, racial, religious, and political determinations are 'mixed' and suspended, and where the transcendent and the immanent (the nation, race, blood, the Ideal) are no longer what grounds our being-in-common. What once was private (taste, feelings) becomes public and the ground for being-together, just as what was public, the ground of the transcendent and the social (the religious, racial, or ethnic) now tends to become private. This is how the foundations of being-together are also being transformed. No longer rigid, stable, universal, or eternal, it becomes fluctuating, mobile, nomadic, plural, and ephemeral. We then witness the the emergence of smaller communities based on extremely fluid ties, temporarily articulated around freely shared passions or feelings. They go back to what Bernard Stiegler calls 'idiomatic, non-territorial communities,' Michel Maffesoli calls 'tribes,' and Hakim Bey thinks of as 'TAZs (Temporary Autonomous Zones).'[26] We have thus entered an era of 'tribes,' networks, and small groups, and live in a time of ephemeral but effervescent gatherings that constitute 'the most accomplished mass expression of creativity.'[27] Today we cannot find a more revelatory example of this creativity—and of the *métissage* produce by today's technics—than techno. As a culture of mixing, it is a de facto and manifest sign of technical and aterritorial coming-into-being, and of the emergence within it of other collective workings. It bears witness to the dual movement affecting and transforming the world today, but shows that this movement, 'a constant back-and-forth established between growing massification and the development of micro-groups'[28] does not in fact reduce 'world-

---

[26] See Hakim Bey, op. cit.
[27] Michel Maffesoli, The Time of the Tribes : The Decline of Individualism in Mass Societies, Sage, 1996. Based on the inversion of polarity between the public and the private that constitutes one of the great paradoxes of our time, Michel Maffesoli asserts that 'the social bond becomes an emotional one,' and that this '"emotionalism" is being affirmed more and more in all the tribes being established in our societies.' Maffesoli, in Au creux des apparences.
[28] Ibid. It may even be that this dual movement Mafessoli refers to here echoes, so to speak, the

globalization' or *métissage* to some amorphous totality bringing everything back to the identical, the same. On the contrary, it creates an opening to the development of a multiplicity of singular differences.

Technics, itself a force of deterritorialization and *métissage*, in its contemporary form effects and provokes this mutation in our being-together, taking it from a belonging in fact (to a nation or a contract) to a polymorphous sociability that no longer recognizes itself in traditional forms of identity. In doing so, it mediates a transfer (or transport) from the religious and ideological to art, in the early Greek sense of *techné*, that is, basing it both on all the diversity of individual techniques and on all the arts. This in turn leads to a profound transformation in our relation to artistic practice. It is no longer subordinated to representation alone, but becomes, so to speak, a way of acting on and in the world, a way of experiencing it and inscribing ourselves in it, singly and collectively, outside any of the political and religious figurations that have fashioned it until now.

We also see how innovative and emblematic of the new attitude toward technics—heralding its capacity for free and creative expression of singularities—the relation of techno to these new technologies is. While it may be legitimate to question whether one can analyze a global situation—today's world in all its political, technical, and artistic dimensions—from the standpoint of one phenomenon, that of techno culture, it does seem that in many respects the latter, by its very constitution, festive and esthetic, is able bearing witness to all the structural upheavals bringing about the metamorphosis of our existential space. We may be in the presence of what sociologists, following Marcel Mauss, call a 'total fact.' Thus, if only because it relates to an attempt at appropriating, then diverting, new technologies in order to create a new environment, no matter how ephemeral, in which to experience

one I analyzed earlier (the withdrawal of the ideological and the utopian as against the opening up to the present). Indeed, 'world-ness' can only come about through such a withdrawal, which is at the same time the enclosure of human territories into closed and antagonistic figures, in the same way that the present-day development of 'micro-groups' proceeds from the rupture, or rather fragmentation, of the social in the shared present or moment.

and share existence in new fashion, techno already bears witness to what constitutes the central issue of the present, both from the point of view of art as well as of politics. This is how the Internet, along with the new attitudes and relationships it presupposes, was born. Deleuze explains that 'it is easy to find a type of machine to correspond to each society, not because machines are determinant, but because they express social forms capable of engendering and using them.'[29] One recognizes in the new technological machines of cyberspace, the Internet and samplers in particular, a surprising desire not only to 'mix' and cross-breed sources of information (sound, visuals, and text), but to make anyone into not just a receiver, but a transmitter and creator. This desire, concretized in new kinds of technical equipment and present in many forms of contemporary artistic practice, permeates in subterranean fashion the whole of the 'body social'—the 'world body'—transforming vertical structures of information and creation into horizontal ones. Thus, for the first time in human history (and this is what makes it a veritable cosmological revolution) the possibility presents itself for every single being to participate actively in the global and horizontal workings of the world. Without harboring any illusions about the 'global village' (which we know at bottom is only the hidden side of economic 'ultra-individualism,' camouflaged under the need for a good conscience on the part of planetary free-market democracy), it cannot be denied there is something like a seismic tremor, slow but spreading throughout the world, from the fissures of which new attitudes, both singular and collective, emerge, converging in the tendency to horizontality and *métissage* (with all the tensions of identity this may provoke) we have been describing.[30]

Technics is deconstructing and reconstructing the space of the world in a dual movement. On one hand, its exponential development (through the ethnic-technics conflict and the concomitant process of deterritorialization we described earlier) has indeed abrogated the

[29] Gilles Deleuze, Claire Parnet, *Dialogues,* New York, 1989.
[30] As we have seen with the Internet and particularly the Web, the 'key is not in the technological level or novelty, but the openness or horizontality of the structure.' Hakim Bey, *op. cit.*

regime of Ideologies and is directing it to its 'end.' On the other, in this very abrogation technics itself emerges as the meaning of existence, an existence that no great figure of Meaning or Truth (Idols, Icons, or Ideologies) can shelter any longer from its lack of essence. Here, technics becomes confrontation, taking on an existence that is no longer sheltered, simulated, or at work. This does not mean there is no longer any work, but simply that that work—the work of technics, but also, and especially, that of art—is no longer representation of what shelters (Truth and all the various declensions of 'one-way' Meaning: God, Nature, Progress), but commitment and the acceptance of existence in the horizontal sharing of its lack of essence. The work of an out-of-work existence opens up a space for that sharing where art and the political can meet, not for fusion but for dialogue. As has long been obvious in techno, we realize that art is indeed not meant to be separate from the political, as if they designated two heterogeneous fields of operations. They are virtually welded to each other in collective articulations, flexible and ephemeral, that form around common sensations. As Nicholas Saunders put it in *E for Ecstasy*, techno is 'communism applied to the emotions.'[31]

Such a convergence of art (taken in the sense of art and technics) and the political does not, however, mean a mere estheticizing of the political (the community as artwork was also the project of fascism) nor even the politicizing of art (we have seen how social or critical art plays along with the power structure it denounces as much as those whom it serves). This may lead us to realize we should at least reflect on, perhaps even welcome, this correspondence between art and the political. But we need to craft an art which is no longer merely a representation of the Ideal, a technics whose finality does not reside exclusively in economic imperatives, and a political space not grounded in some Truth.[32] This constitutes a program that reposes on the possibility of inventing, singularly and collectively, an existence that no

[31] Nicholas Saunders, *Ecstasy: Dance, Trance and Transformation*, Quick Trading, 1996.
[32] This commit us, as Hannah Arendt summoned us to long ago, to become 'aware of the non-political, abd virtually anti-political, nature of the truth.' *The Crisis of the Republic*, New York, 1972.

longer diverts from its own 'finitude' or from its free deployment
within the horizons of the 'worldness,' cross-bred and deterrito-
rialized, offered to us at present. With all due respect to the defenders
of the purity of the Ideal, this may well be, for our time and those of
'us' that share it, both our task and our fate. We turn to art as we
would to our most intimate capacity to maintain and establish ourselves in the absence of any theologico-political foundations. To its
'plastic force,' as Nietzsche[33] would say, as if that might be the only
possibility for us to confront finite existence without taking refuge in
the usual religious and ideological backwaters. When we refuse to
have recourse to the whole panoply of utopian and idealist narcotics,
we are much better able to take the exact measure of how much 'art is
what happens to us (to us Occidentals) par excellence, what offers us
our destiny or what disturbs our history.'[34] This may be indeed be the
history of the event, or the advent, of art, and in it of a human
existence restored to wholeness, so to speak, but of an art which
would—or could—no longer be a 'service' to—or in the service of—
either the Good, the Beautiful, or any other Ideal. Furthermore, the
fact that art has henceforth discovered itself to be—following what
Hegel imagined as the 'end of art'—that which has somehow come to
occupy the vacant space left by the theologico-political, consequently
coming closer to life (as is attested in various ways by so many of the
practices of contemporary art) does not necessarily mean it has lost
either its specificity or symbolic function, nor that it will likely melt
or disappear into life or the everyday. It is not so certain that 'in order
the preserve the freedom acquired in the modern age, contemporary
art [should] once again mark its distance from the world; not, to be
sure, in order to turn away from it, but in order not to melt into it, to
fully assume its function as a symbolic putting-in-perspective.'[35] It
may not be art melting and turning into the world, being somehow
absorbed into the political. On the contrary, it may be the world and

[33] See Friedrich Nietzsche, *The Birth of Tragedy Out of the Spirit of Music/Or, Hellenism and Pessimism*, Leipzig, 1872. Elsewhere Nietzsche says that 'we have art so as not to die of Truth.'
[34] Jean-Luc Nancy, *Une Pensée finie.*
[35] Catherine Millet, *L'Art Contemporain, Paris, 1997.*

the political that is turning into art, broadening its range of operations and exploration far beyond its one 'function as a symbolic putting-in-perspective' and representation.

Techno as an Artistic Laboratory of the Present
From Representation to Participation and Presentation

The Dislocation of the Stage

In the final analysis, mixing, the technique of 'cut-copy-paste' which defines the esthetics of techno with respect not only to its music, but also its flyers[36], modes of dress, and parties, seems to be a mark of our time. This is the exact opposite of the traditional conception of art, which requires of any work that it be pure and finished, as well as autonomous and eternal. To the extent that techno music must each time be replayed, mixed and remixed, in effect interpreted, it produces what Umberto Eco has called an 'open work.' Because it is infinitely interpretable and not locked into a definitive or determined form, techno leads us to reconsider and rethink the notion of a work within the horizons of mobile, moving, and nomadic forms no longer meant to be conceived as a closure of that work, but as a field of experiences and possibilities. What Eco says about the contemporary music of Stockhausen, Berio, or Boulez also holds for techno: 'by making the openness proper to any work a conscious end of its creation, art today confronts us with productions which are not works in the traditional sense,' so that 'we no longer stand before works that ask to be rethought or re-experienced in a particular structural

---

[36] The flyers that announce raves (date, place, time, Djs) are techno's only iconographic support.

direction, but works that their interpreter completes at the moment he undertakes their mediation.'[37] In the end, instead of works what we have is, as Adorno put it, 'paradigms of a possible music.' In contemporary art, too, there is also a slippage from the notion of an artwork to that of an art-object which no longer lays claims to the perfection and eternity of a work, that is to say, which explicitly renounces any closure or definitive completion.

Here one realizes the importance of the DJ, who is no longer someone who simply executes the work, but also and above all its performer and creator. One of the central characteristics of techno music lies in the great freedom afforded its performers, the DJs. For the DJ no longer only has to play or interpret the work, but also has the possibility of profoundly modifying its very structure. This is what the French DJ Jérôme Pacman has in mind when he says, 'You can no longer use the term "disc jockey." A DJ is more of a record-pusher, like someone who runs and organizes a team. For us the musical segments are not an end in themselves. We manipulate them, we work them from the inside, we graft them and ungraft them. We mix them, we drop in sounds, sometimes rain, other times wind, marbles or hail.'[38]

Because he is not just someone who executes a work he only has to play on a turntable, not just a 'record-pusher,' the DJ has a peculiar status. Does that make him an artist, a creator, or, as some have described him, 'a new technological hero' or 'musical shaman'? Whatever he is, his musical activity calls into question our notion of the artist, in the same way that his productions or mixes call into question that of the artwork, its uniqueness, completed perfection and lasting quality. Its productions are no longer encased in an eternally defined structure; the same piece of techno music may be replayed many times without its initial structure being preserved or respected. This is the permanent structural transformation that techno operates on all its productions.

[37] Umberto Eco, *The Open Work*, Cambridge, 1989.
[38] In « Digraphe » n° 68.

It presupposes that musical creation rests more on an open process than on what it produces, as if the works only have value as a stage or support to push the creative process further along. In the end what counts is creation; the fetishizing or sacralizing of the work, instead of contributing to the development of art, is just another form of its neutralization and its reification into commodity spectacle. In this sense, art is not, or no longer, a spectacle requiring disinterested contemplation, as tradition has always had it. Rather, it designates a process that invites participation, and for techno a participation through the body, for it always has been and remains music to dance to.

In this, techno harks back to the festive intensity of traditional societies for whom art was always *fête* and *fête* an art, and where every artistic practice converges in the crucible of the festive, in the heat of which the prohibitions and demands of the social order dissolve, its participants drawn into an ecstatic and cathartic waltz.[39] Furthermore, just as in those societies, here, too, all the arts are mobilized (music, obviously; architecture, painting, and sculpture in the decoration of the inverted space; video, photography and projection of computer-generated images in the production of a visual space), each contributing towards creating a propitious context for the *fête*. Indeed, the point is to create a global context more than a work, unless the work is understood to mean the realization of a space, its collective appropriation, and its sharing.

In the final analysis, the question is no longer one of representation or exposition, but of the genesis of an event to be experienced in common and thereby replayed within a new perspective. To outside observers techno will present only its 'cortex,' its outer skin, if they fail to see this demand for participation and communion of bodies in and through dance. One might also add that unlike other musical events such as rock, punk, or rap, with techno the music never stops;

[39] It is with this in mind that Sergei Bugaev (Africa), one of the artists who introduced techno into Russia at the beginning of the 90s, asserts, 'In the past, the various branches of culture (music, song, painting) tended to gather around the church altar. Today they gather in night clubs.' Interview with Michel Gaillot, in the Saint-Petersburg culture magazine *Pulse*, February, 1996.

it is played or mixed continuously, without the slightest pause, not even when the DJs change. The difference is even greater if one compares it to shows where the audience watches passively. You have the artists, the active ones, on one side, performing for a public on the other side who is supposed to receive and enjoy them without being able to break through the bounds that separate them from the creative process in any way whatsoever. Furthermore, there is no 'spectacu-larizing' of the DJ in raves. They are not up on some stage, before a passively concentrating public ready to receive the spectacle they are offered. DJs are not even announced or introduced, nor are they applauded for their performance; most of the time we do not even see them.

They do not consider themselves artists, even less stars (which was an especially important point in the beginning). They refuse 'aura,' as attested by the widespread anonymousness in the movement. Techno is a world without masters or idols, unlike rock music, where indivi-duality is emphasized, even deified. With the popularization and coop-tation of the movement, we are, however, starting to see a progressive but very real change in direction. Thus, the practice of appropriation and diversion, which in the beginning always sought to take care of its own production, publicity, and distribution, is in turn itself being reappropriated, as if in the end nothing can break the vicious circle of mercantile activity.

Techno would like to break with the traditional conception of art as representation and as a set of dichotomies between creation and reception, and works and their contemplation, as if a relation to the work necessarily required or demanded a purely disinterested and passive esthetic judgment. The fact that techno only can only exist through a demand to participate is significant on the esthetic and artistic level. First of all in relation to the 'artists,' the DJs, who are not the only actors; also to the spectators, the ravers, who are in fact no longer just spectators, but become actors themselves, participants in an event put on not only before and for them, but also, and above all, with them. It is not just the DJ's mixing, but the rave itself that makes the work. This makes for an experience of co-creation and 'co-esthesia' nourished by the contributions of all the participants, artists and public, DJs and ravers, who together become the creators of the collective living sculpture.

In the end, this total participation is the basis and condition for the possibility of techno, its internal requirement. But there is also the the realization of a community in action, a being-together no longer based on contractual or utilitarian imperatives. As such it realizes the end of the *fête*, of art, and of music in its Dionysiac essence, that is, not representation but collective participation and communing at a common event. In this sense, a rave, or even a night out at a club, is the precondition for 'getting into the music' and 'letting go,' body and soul. To be appreciated techno needs to be listened to, lived, danced, and shared in a space specially equipped to receive a group gathered for a *fête* around sound and its distinct rhythms. By all reports, this is just what happens. The great majority of 'techno-philes' admit they only began to appreciate the music during raves. Prior to being experienced in common at those raves, it had no particular effect on them. It is also significant that, when asked about their interest in techno, a number of them report that before they started going to raves they couldn't stand the music. The fact that they make a point of their repulsion to the music itself shows how it can only be appreciated on site and in action at places equipped for shared listening and dancing. It also shows the degree to which it is a festive music for groups. This does not mean that it cannot be listened to or appreciated in solitude or isolation. Yet even here, it takes the listener back to the feelings and sensations experienced during the raves, which, like a rite of initiation, imprint in the participants traces of intensity that leave them open to their further influence.

It is an essentially group and festive music played at high volume and accompanied by lighting effects and smoke machines, often by drugs, whether ecstasy or others. Because its repetitive rhythms act directly on the body, drawing it into dance, techno is akin to trance music, or at least creates the conditions for triggering it. It engenders

sensations which the rationalizing and functionalizing of activity in
modern societies have progressively eliminated or made to disappear.
Techno thus goes back to the Dionysiac, or what Plato in the *Phædrus*,
referring to mystic rites and madness, called the 'telestic' essence of
music, that is, its intimate and natural connection with trance and the
depths of the human soul or psyche. As Philippe de Félice puts it,
'Music is in and of itself, if not an appeal to unconsciousness, at least
an invitation to a dream to which one abandons oneself while
remaining awake, and during which the depths of our being emerge,
the unexpressed possibilities of the strangely confused world we carry
within us. This explains why it is particularly apt to create, beyond
individual divergences, collective states where identical tendencies that
are slumbering can mix and melt together.'[40] This 'strangely confused
world' into which music puts down its roots brings humans back to
their common situation, one where they are no longer wrapped up in
themselves or separated by intangible limits that create identities only
relations of contract can bring into relation. It is a bit as if music led
back to to that 'originary' immanence, to that '*Ur*-One' Nietzsche
speaks of in *The Death of Tragedy*, the Dionysian depth where 'the
spirit of music becomes akin to the very voice of the diffuse but
universal wish in all beings,' to an appeal to the 'primitive unity' from
which all individuals have detached and separated. This is what makes
Nietzsche say that 'music is the Dionysian mirror of the world.'[41] For
him we cannot understand Greece or the West at its birth if we do not
take seriously this 'Dionysian spirit,' passed along to us from the
'mystic and sensual religions' of the East, particularly in music. When
we assert that techno parties are in some sense the Dionysia or bacchanalia of modern times, it is because the West, despite its formidably
rationalized and highly technological structures, has not completely
worked through its mourning for Dionysos, that 'god of the interior,'
as Marcel Detienne has called him, that 'spirit of music' who of
necessity links it to trance, or, as Socrates says in responding to
Phædrus, to 'delirium' ('The greatest good has come to us through

---

[40] Philippe de Félice, *Foules en délire, extases collectives*, Paris, 1947.
[41] Nietzsche, *op. cit.*

delirium [*mania*].)[42] It is no accident that one of the meanings of 'rave' is 'to be delirious.' Techno brings out this 'strangely confused world' not only in each individual, but in a West that thought it had been eradicated once and for all, alive and possible only in societies it ethnocentrically called 'underdeveloped.'

In fact, because of all the arts it is the one that most directly affects the sensibility and emotions, music does not have to communicate meaning (text, message, or verbal ritual) in order to move and exceed the limits of the 'musicked.' It communicates itself all by itself as meaning, communicating without the mediation of language. with that strange power it has, or is, to open single beings up to the sharing of a communion. There in lies its contagious and spellbinding power, its 'refrain,' as Deleuze and Guattari call it, capable of provoking the most extreme deterritorializations, beginning with that most intimate and special one, that of 'self.'

In raves everything is in place to favor this temporary self-effacement, to allow the participants to enter into a trance. The smoke machines and light shows, the permanently reverberating music at high volume, so loud the lowest bass sounds are perceived by the whole body, not just the ears, all help create the most favorable conditions possible for an experience of communion through dancing. To this should be added the fact that since spaces for raves are mostly made up of dance-floors, ravers who go all night little by little lose any sense of time or place, replaced by a kind of commonly shared equilibrium. 'Those who are really out there flock around the totem poles of speakers, heads caught in the rush of decibels. All around them, there's exaltation—the jolting movement, arms jerking spasmodically, hips convulsing, feet and ankles twirling to the syncopated rhythms, with the epileptic hip-hopping that is the sign of the raver.'[43] Giving us that chance at something so starkly shared is doubtless the source of techno's great attraction and power to polarize. 'Avalance, will you take me with you in your fall?—Baudelaire.

[42] Plato, *Phædrus*, 244 a.
[43] Vincent Borel, in *Newlook*, December 1994.

Although this is not unlike much artistic experimentation of the past and present, whether one thinks of attempts to go beyond representation and its privileged spaces, galleries and art centers, or of movements like happenings, Dada, or Fluxus, we soon realize that there is no explicit political position taken with respect to society, nor is there, or has there ever been, for that matter, either a desire or claim on the part of techno to constitute an avant-garde, and thus to replay what happened in art. Here the festive is an end without finality, desired only for itself, as is the sharing or collective experience it temporarily gives rise to. That said, when compared to traditional spectacle (and to all the aforementioned subversive art-forms), techno seems to elude, or replace, the logic of representation, as if there were no longer anything—Truth, Idea, or Form—to be represented, or even proposed, as if we were renouncing the very artistic apparatus that holds there to be an active subject on one hand, and spectators or viewers, passive subjects, mere receivers, on the other.

This bring up the question of the 'scenic,' the stage and its space, which in techno is played out quite differently. It can be shown that the workings of the stage/hall arrangement originated in the altars of the Judeo-Christian West. Such a dichotomy, with its strict separation between the priest, the voice of God, who alone is active, and the faithful, passive and disposed to receive the Truth, has repercussions even today in the way we conceive and lay out art spaces, or viewing spaces in general. There is always a central axis that draws an impermeable and intangible line of separation between stage and hall, artists and spectators, creative activity and contemplative passivity, the work and its reception, and, in the final analysis, between art and life.

Indeed, an entire world—ours, that of the West—is delineated around this vertical axis which demarcates itself from the horizontality of paganism, as we see in traditional and archaic social forms without either such a dichotomy or all the ramifications around which that world was composed and concentrated. It split off from the East, and ultimately, in this respect, from all the other great continental formations of humanity, Africa, Asia, and America. Yet at its birth in ancient Greece some five centuries before the common era, the East, in the figure of Dionysus, still resonated, so to speak, in an rising or emerging West not yet cleft along that bipolar axis which, by separating the world into a 'Beyond' and a 'Here-Below,' prepared the way for Judeo-Christianity and the staging for its representation, to which art has been subordinated until today. It is for this reason, as both Nietzsche and Hölderlin[44] demonstrated in their analyses of Greek theater, particularly tragedy, that we must not minimize or exclude the tension in Greek tragedy between those two worlds, 'the proper [to Greek]' and 'the stranger' in Hölderlin, and the 'Apollonian' and 'Dionysian' for Nietzsche.[45] There both the verticality of representation and the horizontality of participation were intimately knit and joined, even though we have chosen to retain and privilege only the Apollonian side, that of formal Beauty. And there, beyond what was represented always lay a communion of the public in and around dance and music.[46] Comparing, or at least connecting the festiveness of techno and Greek theater also connects us to the furthest reaches, so to speak, the two extremes, of the West, both at its birth and now, no doubt, at its end, as it tends once again to cross-breed, globalize, and hybridize with the rest of the world, in some sense to dissolve into or merge with it. We can now better understand the reasons for the appearance of raves, these contemporary Dionysia, with their festive and participatory coloration. But it also explains why in them Meaning is once again called into question, and how in its very vacillation there opens up a range of new experiments and experiences, a set of new artistic and political horizons that still remain to be explored, inhabited, and shared.

By removing the stage from the participatory experience thus

[44] Hölderlin, 'Observations on Tragedy.'
[45] Nietzsche, *op.cit.*
[46] Although we cannot develop the point in greater detail here, we can at least wonder whether the principal effect of tragedy, what since Aristotle has been called catharsis, the shared and contagious purging of the violence (*hybris*) inscribed in each and every one of us, does come as much, if not more, from the participatory rather than the representational aspect of the dramas, which were also great festive occasions.

initiated, techno breaks with the traditional conception of the space of
representation as it has structured the majority of artistic experiences
and their exhibition in the West. The entire apparatus of the *mise-en-
spectacle* is thereby shaken. Indeed, once there is no longer any
privileged space, no more 'spectacular altar,' so to speak, there is also
no longer a center toward which looking can be directed and focused.
The centering and centralizing characteristic of representation exhausts
itself in the participatory decentering in a collective experience of the
'work,' and as a 'work.' This desire on the part of techno to do without
not just the stage, but the whole idea of the hall, the theater, and other
traditional sites of the spectacle, is no accident. Just as it has for
growing numbers of contemporary artists, it has now become clear that
in order to get beyond the vertical logic of pure representation that
keeps the public separated from the experience of active participation
in art, it was necessary to concretely, materially, leave behind the places
devoted to art and spectacle.[47] This could in many respects also help
create resistance to the absorption and commodity reification through
which the market and the social system reappropriate what is evolving
around their edges and reinsert it into the economic circuit. They can
even make their own opponents into a means of protection, while
allowing them to preserve their good conscience that they permit
something that's different from, even opposed to, themselves. It is no
doubt in this devious dialectical process that rock itself was anes-
thetized, neutralized, and transformed into a merely cultural phenomenon. The decentering and horizontality of the participatory experience
of the work is a profound upheaval of the very structure of esthetic
reception, if only because it takes us from an optical relation to art to a

---

[47] We do not claim that in situ, as Daniel Buren called it, or site-specific work, that is, the creation or presentation of a work in the world, in social space, or in private spaces like apartments,
and not just in spaces devoted to art (as if art were only possible in such spaces) constitutes a
definitive answer to the problem of representation. Nor that the 'participation' of the viewer in
the work can in some way resolve the social and political problems we face today. It is obvious
that so many site-specific or participatory works, even when they attempt to go beyond staging
and representation, are at times no more that sad parodies of that openness of and in the work
to an experience of sharing. Indeed, in their desire to replace social existence by abandoning the
usual art-spaces, they often do no more than displace the logic of representation from one space
to another, doing nothing more that mimicking or simulating that openness.

haptic one.[48] As a consequence, what links people in this experience is no longer based on a solitary and passive contemplation, but on the collective and actively motivated involvement of all the senses, everything that touches and is touching, including vision (but no longer exclusively). Here, too, one of the great pillars of the scenic apparatus of Western esthetics is shaken. Vision—the primacy of the optical—no longer takes up or absorbs the whole of art, which can now be recomposed of and by the other senses. The body is once again mobilized, engaged, and shared in its totality. There is also the possibility for the work to dematerialize and be transformed into the shared experience of a complex constellation of emotions and sensations. And then art is no longer something that creates artworks, not even art-objects. It is no longer a spectacle, either of the world or of itself, in this respect breaking with its own autonomy (the modernity of 'art for art's sake') through which it had emancipated itself from its service function. What is created is no longer a work in the traditional sense, since there is no finished form. It is rather a situation, an event, or the prelude to an experience of sharing, in which the artist is involved and implicated with, and not just across from, his public, just like the DJs in a rave.

Contemporary art as the Experience of and Demand for a 'With.'

This makes the artist into not just the creator of an art situation, but something like its initiator, a 'runner' of life situations and contexts which are then taken over collectively. In other words, it no longer represents the world, nor even art, but presents it, while letting the plurality or multiplicity of singular beings that inhabit it speak. In these participatory experiences, and in the demand that drives them

[48] See also the discussion of this issue in the interview with Michel Maffesoli in the present volume. In this respect, art transcends all the criteria that once allowed us to judge it. Elsewhere Maffesoli states, 'There may be nothing to say, or not much to communicate, but the important thing in make visible that invisible drive to exchange, the desire of viscosity.' In Michel Maffesoli, Au creux des apparences.

to give voice or speech to the singular—again, to present them, not represent them—we are witnessing a veritable upheaval of the usual givens of art, and of its exhibition and reception. The viewers or spectators become actors, just as the artists also become spectators. Consequently, what makes for the work and the meaning of the work no longer depends on what it communicates or addresses, but on itself, in that it invites us to an experience no longer based on isolation and separation, but on sharing and participation. This had already been undertaken in art with the happening, where spectators had been invited to take part, no longer just in the experience of reception, but also and above all in the creation of the work. What had been something of an insider phenomenon with happenings, which began in the '60s with the actions of Allan Kaprow, today, or at least since about ten years ago—about the same time as raves began—tends to constitute an important and central part of the the ongoing experimentation in contemporary art. Here we are thinking of all those actions during which artists propose events or situations to be experienced collectively, or a situation to be taken over in common, as if the artists were there only to initiate the sharing, as if the work itself were in the end only the actuality and intensity of that sharing. There are many artists whose work could be cited here, typified by Dan Graham or Claude Lévêque, but rather than providing lists of names, we prefer to focus on the various tendencies they represent. It is in the tending toward a replacement of representation with participation, of verticality with horizontality, that we are now seeing the emergence of a 'political' experience in art. This is a break with the classic and modern conception of art as representation, as a dichotomy between creation and reception, and between works and their contemplation, as if the latter necessarily required a disinterested and passive, disincarnate and optical esthetic judgment.

If this is changing, if through this horizontality of participation spectators are placed not only before the work, isolated from creation, but become actors, so to speak; if, therefore, there is a space to be invested in common, and thereby a political experience through and in art, it is because representation itself is running on 'empty,' on 'nothing,' no longer having either Image, Idol, or Idea to (re)present as a foundation and cement of the common and the community.[49] As Jean-Luc Nancy has shown, today art 'is not longer doomed to the servility of representation, but destined for the liberty of presentation and the presentation of liberty—for offering.'[50] In this sense art opens up into—and implicates 'us' as it does so—a space for that horizontality, one where nothing, no given or produced meaning, can any longer provide a ground or be a scene on stage, whether that of art or of society. It is, however, experience and event, opening up into a sharing of the surpassing or exceeding by the 'with' and the 'we' of the forms trying to represent it. It is as if the plurality of this originating ontological layer of being-together could be appropriated by or reduced to the One only arbitrarily. Art is precisely the fracture and fragmentation of that Unity. By leading us back to polymorphous and irreducible plurality, it commits us to leaving open the 'between' of humans, not to filling it with the True, the Good, or the Beautiful, and thereby allowing us the mourning of that Total Beauty into which we have always attempted to resorb it, and which is only the other side of Totalitarianism.

To put it perhaps a bit too schematically, art, after gaining its freedom, its 'autonomy,' in the modern age ('art for art's sake'), after a long tradition of art as religious or political 'service,' once again tends to return to the world, to rejoin life, and to 'care' for it, perhaps not in order to improve it, but more modestly to engender and invent collective experiences of sharing no longer based on the usual mythological and ideological foundations that have supported and figured it until now. This is an all the more urgent task now that those foundations, in their very obsolescence, have laid bare the layer of being-together that is not operable or cannot be figured. This is perhaps the sense of contemporary art, the active engaging in the opening up of meaning, or to put it another way, the experience of sharing of existence at the very level of the 'ungrounded ground' of meaning.[51]

[49] Techno's muteness, its refusal of slogans and messages, is perhaps nothing more than saying this 'nothing.'
[50] Jean-Luc Nancy, *Une Pensée finie.*
[51] In one way, this participatory experience was also present in what was called the Nouveau

But this is not some nihilist adventure, as if it were precisely Meaning or Truth that we were lacking, and we were somehow counting on its coming or return. We need to understand that meaning is not what is lacking, but that the withdrawal of all its historical, religious and political, figures leads us to share it in different fashion, although in a way that always overwhelms any attempt to appropriate it. It is this excess of meaning that art and philosophy are faced with at present. It is also why Catherine Millet can make the somewhat pained assertion that 'the less the artwork refers to some higher truth, aspiration, or reality to come, the more its only function appears to be a social cement (all the more necessary that there is no other). Somehow, the less it indicates a meaning our lives might have, the more we conglomerate around it to fill in the lack with our presence.'[52] In the same way that techno does not create a work but an environment, a situation to be experienced in common, all the collective actions and performance in contemporary art bear witness to a similar need to implicate the public in the flowering of the work, to make it into a political experience, an experience of the 'with'. In sum, art becomes political not as representation, however sublime, of Meaning or Truth, but as experimentation and putting-in-perspective (and prospective) of the political (the experience of 'with'), not of politics (the subordination, figuration, and administration— however enlightened—of the 'with').

We also realize that this is not a time for social or critical art, and that there is no longer the political *engagement* to the great ideological struggles that have driven modernity. But it is not certain we can say that it will thereby become disengaged from or uninterested in the world or fail in its responsibilities. On the contrary, it seems to us that, just as with the ideological muteness of techno, it corresponds to another demand for the political or the 'with,' one no longer based on

Roman. There, too, the reader was invited to give life and body to what was being read. Through this 'participatory reading,' he was imprinting a form on the work which the author had left open and presented as such. Michel Théron speaks of an opposition between '(classical) "representation" and (modern)"presence" or between "art-theater" and "art-ceremony".' Michel Théron, *'Rhétorique et art moderne,'* in *L'Art aujourd'hui,* Paris, 1993.
[52] Catherine Millet, *op. cit.*

the ideological or the utopian. This demand derives from the impossibility of persisting in the eschatological logic of programming or projection of meaning, as well as of the 'with' and of being-together.

It is as if we can no longer entrust ourselves to a truth to come, as if we have realized that the 'with,' shared existence, had no other reality than that of the present. Art tends to take the empty place once occupied by the ideological and the relation it implies. It increasingly becomes what holds us together in the abeyance of all meaning that can be given to the producible.[53] From the moment it is no longer spectacle but event, that is, no longer representation of something but participation in something, the space of the work is radically transformed. It becomes an opening up to the horizontality of participation on the 'ungrounded ground' of inappropriable meaning, that is, of finitude.

This is no doubt the major reason why for several years now, there are more and more artists' proposals conceived as nothing more that possible paradigms for a work, in the sense that they only take form—become art or work—to the extent they are invested, inhabited, and determined by spectators.[54] The relation to the work is no longer based on the contemplation of a finished object, not simply as was the case with performances and Body Art, where there was also a de-materialization and de-reification of the work, but especially because here the work is completed or indeed exists only to the extent that the spectators realize the work in and as an experience of its sharing.

It should be added that this participatory tendency in art tends to rehabilitate, if that is the proper term, a dimension more characteristic of popular art. This would also help explain the connection between

---

[53] It can be shown that it is possible to take all the forms of staging and all the different spaces of representation, from Greek tragedy down to techno and contemporary art, and deduce from them different social and political conceptions that gave rise to them.

[54] For more detail, see Eric Troncy, 'Le Spectateur et l'Accident,' Artpress, n°266, July–August 1997. He relates and analyzes how 'since the end of the '80s certain works have stated their conviction that they are unfinished without the presence of the spectator.

contemporary art and popular culture, namely that of a somatic experience of art where the body, and the sharing of bodies, is longer be eluded or denigrated, and is even promoted. In doing so, contemporary art would be finally be able, far more than politics, to give free reign to our original sociability, that 'with' always expressed in the festive, and experienced today in raves. Raves, like much of contemporary art practice, bear witness to the fact that the body will not allow itself to be confined in private life alone, in that 'minuscule enclosure,' as Bataille called it. It's as if in social space there were a resistance or recurrence of the ineluctable demand to share and have a collective experience.

Because art, like the festive, takes root deep in this original layer of being-together—and the latter is now no longer grounded in the One-and-Only, but in the multiple and in the singular—one can understand why it takes part in participatory experiences where nothing is proposed, neither meaning or truth, but where a collective and corporal sharing can then begin. One cannot hardly deny that delineates a collective putting-into-play of the body reminiscent of the Body Art of the '70s, but which is radically different in that it implies not only the body of the artist, but also and above all that of the viewers, who now are no longer simple viewers, but become real actors. In one sense, Body Art remains derivative of a logic of representation, for on one hand, the very body of the artist tends in effect to be made into an artwork or art-object, incorporating into itself, so to speak, the logic at work in painting or sculpture. On the other, it leads to a process, in the end a very modern and Romantic one, of exacerbating the subjectivity of the artist and making it into something quite sovereign. When the work invites an active participatory experience, it gives rise to a kind of collective Body Art which no longer represents something on or of the body, but which presents it in the efficacy and intensity of its sharing. The sharing of bodies takes on the political and public dimension of and in art. It is no longer the body, or even just bodies, that are being exhibited here, but more precisely their sharing, their being-together—their 'with,' no longer based on something religious or ideological. In other words, it is the 'with' or the 'between' (the 'between' of bodies, of singular beings, sharing itself), in the final analysis the horizon of the Other, that tends to define the operant and exploratory field of art.

As with a growing body of work that forming something of a constellation, though a significant one, within contemporary art (although it cannot necessarily be considered a model or criterion for judging relevance or quality) there is also an increasingly pressing emergence of a need for art that no longer considers itself separate, 'an art apart' hermetically sealed and protected in the 'privileged position' conferred upon it by modernity.[55] In other words, from the reconnection of art to bodies, to other, singular beings, and, in the end, to life in its very presence, it results that art itself should no longer be capable of withdrawing into the categories of 'fine art,' the sublime, or the representation of Idea, Idol, and Ideal which constitute its task. It would surely be a misunderstanding and misconstrual of the nature of this demand to see in the interest more and more artists are showing in popular culture only the wish or need to draw inspiration in sources other than art because the latter no longer provides it. It is because these categorizations have themselves become inoperative and untimely that the impermeability of the line between art and popular culture can no longer be justified, maintained, and preserved. We should realize that the desire to keep art only on the level of a 'fine art' comes only from a reactive wish to disconnect it from life, from existence, singular and collective, isolating it from anything that might allow it to proliferate outside the framework outlined for it by the socio-economic powers that be. It is thus in the name of its very autonomy that we reduce it to a pure and disincarnate esthetics, which for us would be an-esthesia, farce, or commodity-spectacle simulation.

We would be assuredly depriving ourselves of what art had to

[55] Indeed, we are not claiming that 'participation'-art—or 'presentation'-art—is now the only art possible, or the only art of quality, or that in this respect other contemporary forms are obsolete. We are only interested in what is manifests there of the demand taking general hold of the political and cultural fields of our being-in-the-world.

articulate to us if we came to think that the desire being expressed in
it somehow did not concern us directly, or derived in fact only from a
philosophical discourse trying to appropriate it for itself and speak in
its stead. In reality, the factors that have brought about both the
upheaval in art and its opening to the world concern all of 'us,' and it
is in this respect perhaps being called upon to take the deserted place
of religion and the political. That is, it is fast becoming the only
capability we have for sharing and bonding, in the commitment of
our singular and collective existences, since they have been deprived
of all theologico-political foundation. As a result, 'if a certain deter-
mination of 'art,' that is, ours, that of the age that gave 'art' its name,
as such and absolutely, and which may also be coming to an end,
along with that of the 'fine-art' categorizations that come with it, and
with them and esthetic sentiment and judgment, a sublime delecta-
tion,' it may also be the sign of a new task for our art, one where it is
no longer separated from the popular arts, on one hand, or from
technics on the other.[56] Indeed, if it no longer has as a heritage only
the representation of the Idea, but also the sharing of singular bodies
and the presentation of finite existence, technics, in the present-day
figure of new technologies, may come to seem what art is most
intimately concerned with. So intimately that it will tend—as heralded
by its Greek form, *techné*—to merge with it, at least in the sense that
what will now be played out in it, in this age of withdrawal of 'one-
way' Meaning, is nothing less than the the invention of existence in all
its dimensions: singular, collective, corporal, artistic, and technic.

To the extent that today there is nothing left to define existence
other than this new relation to technics, a relation within which
technics self-constitutes itself at the interface between man and
machine to the point where they now interpenetrate each other, we
come to understand that art, too, has an interest in technics. It
appropriates it by diverting it (the way techno itself does) to ends other

---

[56] Jean-Luc Nancy, *Les Muses*. Then, based on this exhaustion, or of the 'end' of this 'determi-
nation of art,' one could 'demonstrate that a formula of the kind "art and/or technics" might
well condense in its own way the enigma of our time.'

than those for which it was intended. Indeed, one one hand the new technologies 'constitute a means. . .well adapted to the work of artists, a tool that favors the decipherment of the grammar of the world, and by virtue of this is a factor for liberty, allowing us to decipher codes, redo them, and reassemble them in different fashion.'[57] On the other, because this interpenetration of man and technics engages our very existence in what is called 'virtual reality,' a new world no longer based on 'being,' but, as Bernard Stiegler has demonstrated, on the 'possible,' art that reclaims technics becomes creative not just of art, but of the world and the existences that are its weave[58]. As a result, since these technologies are in a position to make this new environment for our existences an effective reality (as techno has done by creating a new sound environment), we understand why so many artists are beginning to work with them, even if it must be said that many remain for the moment prisoners of technical performance. It nonetheless remains that a new space for art has opened up, and from which, as happened with cinema, then video, a new artistic form will emerge.

What is most innovative in this artistic appropriation of contemporary technology, especially with respect to virtual technology, is not based, or at least not essentially, on a better means of representing

[57] Patrick Talbot, interview with the artist Piotr Kowalski, in *Artpress*, special issue n°12, on 'New Technologies, 1991. Since here we are unable to analyze in greater detail the new artistic space being opened up by the use of new technologies by artists, I refer the reader to this special issue of *Art-Press*, as well as to the chapter Paul Ardenne devotes to it in his book *L'Art à l'âge contemporain: Une Histoire des arts plastiques à la fin du XXème siècle*, Paris, 1997.
[58] Here we move to another 'paradigm,' that is, where 'science become techno-science no longer deals with the living, but with the 'possible' of the living.' In this sense, science is not what describes being, but what transforms it. 'Our horizon is no longer being, but the possible.'
(Bernard Stiegler, extract from a lecture given at the *Collège Universitaire Français* in 1994 in Moscow. With these technical mutations we are experiencing a veritable cosmological revolution in which our existences have been displaced and transported from the horizon of metaphysics or ontology (that of 'being') to that of the 'possible' or the virtual. With these new communications technologies, along with genetic manipulation, contemporary technics is in a position to develop unheard of possibilities for existence, starting with the augmentation and extension of the real through the virtual, the insertion of life and its sharing into the very heart of this new reality, and the transformation of man himself in the very depths of his most intimate nature, that of his body. Even though we may not yet be in a position to appreciate or fully measure all the consequences, we must nonetheless recognize that this interpenetration of man and technics defines, along with cyberspace, a new global horizon for human existence.

the world, but on an astounding possibility of augmenting or extending it.[59]

With virtual images one is no longer finds oneself frontally across from a wall, a screen, or a surface, but in the presence of a new horizon which one can enter and experience singly and collectively. We are no longer dealing with a copy of the the real or the world, with its representation, but rather with its extension. This gives rise to new sensibilities, as well as to a new mode of being-in-the-world, being-in-the-body, and of sharing. It is existence in its totality that is being replayed in completely new fashion, in that its ontological constitution, from the point of view both of emotions as well as sensations, is modified in passing from 'being' to 'the possible.' Here we may note that 'by the same token as the social machines one can categorize under the general heading of 'collective equipment,' technological machines for computing and communicating operate in the heart of human subjectivity, not only within memory and intelligence, but also within sensibility, affects, and unconscious fantasies.[60] It is in the same sense that Marshall McLuhan and Quentin Fiore affirmed that 'the extension of a single sense organ changes the way we think and act, our perception of the world. When those factors change, human beings are changed, too.'[61]

As a result, the technology which gives rise to this new existential horizon will no longer be merely a supplementary technological gadget to distract art from its present incapacity to produce meaning or make sense, and thereby to prosper in its 'non-sense.' Conversely, since it is human life considered in its integrality that is at stake, art

[59] One could even say that with virtual reality we leave representation behind, for the virtual no longer presents a truth; it is its own truth endlessly engendering itself.' Philippe Quéau, in *Blocnotes*, n°4. In fact, the virtual is neither fictive nor unreal, rather it is constituted as an augmented real. Today the point is no longer, as Descartes had it, 'to become masters and owners of nature,' but to transform, reformulate, and, even more, to extend it.
[60] Félix Guattari, *op.cit.* In this sense, what we call 'wearable computers,' the whole panoply of computerized clothing like digital gloves or cybersuits, extend the human body, grafting a new meaning onto it, so to speak, that allows it to tele-sense and tele-touch, that is, experiment and experience at a distance, in a context that is no longer one of nature or of the natural world
[61] Marshall McLuhan and Quentin Fiore, *The Medium is the Message*, New York, 1966.

that does not concern itself with this issue must admit its incapacity to remain bonded to the real, to the world and the singularities that divide and knit it back together.

The point is not to cede to a 'rhetoric of the technological sublime' where the body no longer carries any weight, where it evaporates and becomes 'obsolete,' as Stelarc seems to think. This is a 'theory of escape velocity, where the body falls away like the first stage of a rocket, while *Homo sapiens* hastens its post-human and pan-planetary evolution.'[62] But as with techno, the new artistic, and more generally existential, practices proffered in this mutation of the world do not cause the body to disappear, but simply displace it, involving it in a new environment.[63] What cross-breeds, merging and emerging, in this nebula of arts and technics, makes up a thickening thread or web of 'horizontality' within which we have to invent a new mode of being-in-the-world, and do so in common. In other words, these practices offer no relief for finitude or for the gaps in horizontality. They can neither fill nor fence them in; quite the contrary, they can only dig deeper, indefinitely replaying it in each work, artistic or technic, in such a way that gives it a chance to proliferate in its multiple and irreducible meaning.

But this means recognizing that the status of the artist has also changed. The latter, through all the upheavals and mutations of his practice, was unable to last in that heroic, sacral, or demiurgic pose assigned him by modernity. From the moment he is no longer that Romantic or sublime figure of genius, ready and able to tap the source of the meaning that is our lot, his authority begins to fade. It is then that what was the great demand of techno, the effacement of the proper name, along with collective activity of creation, became an increasingly frequent practice in contemporary art.[64] This further shakes the emblematic image of the artist, in some sense the last pillar of what makes art

[62] Mark Dery, *Vitesse virtuelle, la cyberculture aujourd'hui*, Paris,1997.
[63] Although it was developed in the crucible of new technologies, techno nonetheless remains opposed to this 'technological sublime,' if only through its insistence on or persistence in taking root in the body, or, to put it more precisely, the active and collective participation of bodies.
[64] As examples one might cite General Idea, Art Club 2000 and Mobil Image.

into a exercise in sovereignty or authority. Yet it is not the artist who is disappearing, but only the exacerbation of his ego or subjectivity. Moreover, in the same way the artist tends to effacement and disappearance in favor of encounter and sharing, the work itself tends to open up as an object, privileging action and relation in the space it proposes to us, that is, the singular experience of communalizing the existence of which it consists. In this questioning of the traditional constitution that opens the work to its public, and more generally to life, the work sheds its sacredness, allowing itself to be inhabited by the multiplicity of the noises of the world and the speech of the singular.

This also explains why artistic practice is becoming increasingly fluid and ephemeral, tending to overflow the traditional framework of art and its presentation. This presents unavoidable difficulties for any institution who does not know how to adapt to this fluidity, or how to present and manage it, frantic at seeing the art slip through its fingers. In the general frenzy provoked by art today—we like to complain that art doesn't reach the broad public, but hasn't that always been the case?—all the traditional signposts for its practice, reception and criticism totter, and may even seem useless for comprehending the situation. As is always the case at moments when situations change and mutate toward other forms and other horizons, the voices of the 'arrière-garde' awaken and begin lamenting about the 'failure' of art, the lack of 'responsibility,' the loss of its 'critical mission,' as if art were in 'crisis,' as if it ought to return to its 'beginnings,' once again to be the 'privileged guarantor of truth' or 'identity.' Or worse yet, that there is an 'art conspiracy.' One can only register one's surprise, if not dismay, at such 'polemics' or 'quarrels,' although they do at least have the merit, in keeping with their reactive, even reactionary, passion, of revealing the depth and breadth of the upheavals affecting contemporary art today. It may be that, quite the contrary, art has never been as rich, diverse, or free as it is right now, just when it no longer has anything to represent, no doubt *because* it no longer has anything to represent. In the end, what makes for the sadness or badness of all those who speculate on the 'crisis' or 'failure' of art today, also constitutes its inexhaustible richness.

****

*T*hus a new artistic continent has been delineated, where, to previously evoked participatory experiences, must be added a plurality of gestures, propositions, and actions that demarcate themselves from the logic of the master narratives of modernity, breaking with a historical and political conception that sees its finality in the project and advent of Meaning and Truth, whether religious, political, or even artistic. It is in this context of the fragmentation and dissemination of One Meaning into multiple Meaning that artistic work we might now call the New Narrativity (Pierre Huyghe) or the New Figuration (Stephan Balkenhol) has taken root. The great narratives and figures of the One have been succeeded by the micro-narratives of the everyday (here one might mention the work of Joel Bartoloméo), in the same way that the singular speech of 'we,' 'us,' the open and exposed 'faces' of 'people' have succeeded the eschatological and authoritarian discourse of Totality and Identity. We are now moving onto something else, to a world no longer confined to authority, no longer violently barricaded behind an identity warranted by ancient shades, divine and ideological. With this engaging of the space of the singular, whether in the New Narration or other artistic practices that radicalize it, like Sylvie Blocher's *Living Pictures*, we note that art now tends to 'depose' its own authority and to 'endorse,' so to speak, to back its 'responsibility,' thus going from a function of 'service' and 'representation' to that of 'presentation.'[65] It no longer represents Meaning, the True, or the Beautiful, but instead presents the irreducible multiplicity of singular existences, or rather invites it to reveal, expose, or express itself there. To choose not to see this closing of an entire history, the History of Modernity and its fathers, but with it the opening of another history, the history of 'us,' 'we' the singular beings who, with the withdrawal of the great Idols and Ideals can only ground ourselves in the heterogeneous and irreducible plurality of our

[65] See the article by Michel Gaillot on the work of Sylvie Blocher, in *Blocnotes* n°12, April–May 1996. It can be shown that the radicality of her artistic or political gesture lies precisely in her introducing 'presentation' into the field of art, thereby causing it to lose its 'authority.'

existences, would be rejecting nothing less than an understanding of what was happening to us, creating our destiny for us, and perhaps even a task for our art, namely the implosion of the world into a multiplicity of fragments or 'punctualities' of existence: 'us.' When the world is us, we notice that the very modalities of dwelling in it and sharing it shift from the Authority and Truth of the theologico-political towards a global space of existence where each of us inherits his or her own responsibility. Since one can no longer commit oneself either to a God or a master, we become as responsible for ourselves as for the world itself. This shift also explains why contemporary art has become increasingly interested in new technologies, for, as we have seen, in them is played out the *mise-en-forme* of our singular and collective existences, of the body proper as well as the body social or the body-world. It is up to us to learn how to dwell in this present—it matters little whether we call it contemporary or postmodern—and to reflect on and welcome the double correspondence it brings with it, one which now weaves the horizontality without ground of our existence: between art and technics, on one hand, and between art and the political, on the other. But we must learn to do so without having recourse to the usual catastrophic estheticizing of the political or the politicizing of art. It is time to realize that it is not the arts that are in 'crisis' or a 'failure,' but the theologico-political world which can longer subordinate or appropriate them for itself. To see in them only the desire for 'nullity' or 'loss of identity' (that of the artist, the public, and the work) would without a doubt leave us in the most blind and vain position one can take today: where, blind to what is coming, 'we' are no longer able to see that it has already happened to us, and that what is coming about, in another form and at another time, in another space and with another lot, is the world itself in its globality. And this is what we are the contemporaries of, 'we,' the heirs without a testament, the orphans of One-Way Meaning. 'Neither God nor Master' was already reserved for us, foreseen by Nietzsche a century ago, like a gift of speech pre-addressed, to 'us,' who, lightened of all our fathers, already have one foot outside the West, the one on which we dance to the techno sound of our Dionysiac present.

An Interview with Jean-Luc Nancy

Innovative in its esthetics (the 'mix'), in its relationship to new technologies, and in the way it positions itself with respect to the political, techno nonetheless preserves a certain archaic aspect, 'archoriginal,' so to speak, to the extent that in it there subsists, or rather resurges, behavior peculiar to the 'festive,' in the general sense (Dionysia, bacchanalia, the carnival, etc.), as we see it at work in traditional societies. Do you think that these behaviors or tendencies have somehow exhausted themselves, or become anesthesized—at least in the West? Haven't they become reified into leisure or commodity spectacle, that is, into mere spectacles where the fête, the festivity, has lost its power of bonding and sharing, and in one sense is no more than a mere parody of itself—or, to use the Situationist vocabulary, a 'simulation' or 'simulacrum'?

I must first point out that I am totally incompetent as far as the technique and esthetics of techno are concerned. I have no hearing or vision, nor any technical knowledge of what it represents. That aside, I would say the way you put the question immediately poses a problem for me. You said 'innovative in its esthetics, techno nonetheless preserves an archaic aspect,' and then asked, 'Isn't it this archaic aspect of traditional festivals that had exhausted itself, and is now reappearing or being brought back?' But I wonder whether that opposition between 'innovative' and 'archaic,' linked by 'nonetheless'—as if innovation couldn't somehow be archaic—isn't something that should be questioned from the start. Because even when I try to envision what you said, a certain 'return of the archaic,' why must it be thought of as happening 'despite innovation'? Shouldn't we be asking whether innovation isn't precisely what is needed, not in order for the archaic to return, but to cast into a new light something that in fact belongs to an order, layer, or stratum fundamental to experience? Then, with respect to that 'nonetheless,' consider, if you will, the hypothesis that there is in fact a great deal of cohesion between innovation and what you call 'archaism' (although perhaps, rather than calling it archaic, it would be better to call it 'archoriginal,' something that has never taken place, will perhaps never take place, but which underlies our whole experience of being-together.

Well, that's something like what I meant when I said the innovation of techno lay in the capacity it has, or is, to bring back, or into a new light.

I agree with you there. But it's important to stress the link between innovation and this 'return'—the return as itself something new, the return of the new, or of something that has never taken place. Perhaps that means the real question we should be asking is, 'What is it that risks, or might risk, being nothing but 'return,' and thus, nostalgia [*Nostos* in Greek means 'return.'—*Trans.*], a nostalgia for things tribal and archaic, for the idea that there may have been something like an unmediated *fête*—when, as you point out, there is in all the archaic festivals we know of a sacred dimension missing in techno. So we cannot go on speaking of 'return'; otherwise it would be, as you imply towards the end of your question, a parodied or simulated return, the return of a simulated sacred.

This said, I would make another observation, given the conditions we have just outlined: Yes, there is something like 'return,' but I think this something is not strictly proper to techno. It is contemporary with rock, in more than one respect, even. But for me it's a very difficult question, because I myself am no doubt insufficiently contemporary with rock music. I grew up and lived in a completely different climate and social milieu. I only became familiar with rock music much later, when it had already become a cultural phenomenon. Rock seems to me an undeniably enormous phenomenon. It is not a coincidence that it began and developed at the same time as another kind of great convulsion, of our society and civilization, began and developed. And at one particular moment, in 1968, it caused a rupture in many areas. So in one way, I have a hard time seeing any difference between rock and techno. Obviously I also tend (though at some remove, based on what I may have heard elsewhere and also perhaps because of my age) to think of techno as a degeneration of rock, a musical degeneration. And also perhaps a degeneration in that rock once seemed to (and did, in certain respects) bring with it commitment and a certain message.

It's true that on the last point there is an important difference. And that's I why formulate my question around the esthetic innovativeness of mixing, which doesn't strictly speaking come out of rock, which was rather opposed to the empire of the machine, or its political position, since techno doesn't have a message and distances itself from any ideology, the exact opposite of rock.

I'm not so sure about that, since rock doesn't seem that opposed to the machine. It quickly took up the use of electric instruments, even if it didn't in fact use mixing or sampling. And at the same time, it used the machine in its sound—the guitar, among other things—and also in the acoustic amplification at concerts. One might even say that the most innovative of all, even before rock, was jazz, as it came to be played by small ensembles.

Yes, that was very innovative, because jazz, and then rock, at least at first, before they both became cultural phenomena, both brought out this festive power.

Right.

There are many similarities, but the main point that differentiates techno from rock in this context is the lack of a position, of commitment, or of any ideological and political demands, and therefore of an appeal to any kind of communitarian development. You don't have any of that in techno, and despite all that, as I said, it nonetheless preserves an archaic aspect that calls on the original source of being-in-common. In this sense it seems to me in these festivals, in raves—contrary to what we are told most of the time—some kind of common space and time opens up where it's as if individuals, through the music or the dancing, or because of the singular and unusual context of these fêtes, are siphoned into a 'with,' a 'together,' or a 'share' other than the one that usually binds them to social space.

I, too, would say these feasts of communal intoxication, of breaking away from the conditions of everyday life, of intoxication in the broad sense of the term, 'enthusiasm,' in a shared space, as you call it, sharing nothing, perhaps, but a space and time removed from our daily servitude, have always occurred. When you mention archaic feasts, one could say this archaism has always been present in popular or folk festivals and town dances. And although it now seem quite ridiculous to speak of 'dances', I think just the same that these dances, like the celebrating on

Bastille Day, for example, still partake of it. But let us see if we can express more precisely what has happened to this general festivity, since I quite agree that some lack of it must have been felt, which engendered or released something that with rock became much more visible than before. But a lack of what, given that there have always been dances and festivals? I think that now it might come from the fact that the festive is less and less inscribed within a ritual framework. There is a general social ceremonial, one which definitely cannot be considered separate from religious and familial feasts, First Communions, weddings, funerals, as well as dances and fairs. The more one tries to describe all of this with some precision, the more one is drawn back into a world that is rural or based in the village, where you have the market-fair and parish feasts, along with something more familiar we are so quick to make jokes about, namely the tournaments, whether bowling or *boules*, or the picnics sponsored by the local fishing club, or whatever. Most of these things continue to exist and I'm sure they still have role to play.

But doesn't all that tend to be transformed into leisure?

I completely agree that a portion of it has been drawn into leisure, but another portion of it has, I think, been preserved along with its ritual and repetitive role. But at the same time the general framework of this rituality has disappeared. It may have disappeared for two major reasons: one is the disappearance of religious frameworks along with all the religious feasts; the second is an overwhelming tendency toward the disappearance of rural society, and with it the fact that things no longer happen in small social units like villages.

But conversely, can it not be said this is linked to an increase in leisure, as well as to the commercial exploitation of that leisure—a 'spectacular' exploitation consisting of the absorption of those festive zones into leisure and their integration into an economic logic.

Yes, O. K. But I just meant that while I am not opposed to speaking of 'commercial exploitation' or 'spectacular commodity,' I would like to bring in some qualification. Of course the market and the market economy that profits from everything has taken over this along with everything else. . .

That's how rock was spent. . . .

Yes, rock was obviously spent that way. But that makes for great difficulties for the effectiveness of techno, for it is very difficult to grasp techno in childbirth, and still virginal with respect to the market. Very, very quickly—as soon as it arose—it has already been drawn in.

I'm not so sure that's generally true. In the beginning, at least, it was something outside all of the traditional sites of spectacle. . .

Yes, as far as the festiveness of the rave goes. But what about the music itself?

As far as the music goes, people started these small record labels and produced their own music, just as punk did, I think, in order not to have to deal with the record industry and the big companies.

Yes, but what I meant is that commodity exploitation is one thing, you could say, but that which makes it possible is another. We must admit that we are in a period which has recognized there was no such thing as a socialist economy, or in any case there hasn't been one. It's not a socialist economic system, or a political one, for that matter, that collapsed. There was no socialist economy; there was just state capitalism, a monopoly capitalism of the state. I absolutely do not mean that everything about the market is good, nor that we should justify or praise the market because there is nothing else. But I do think that for us, the question of capitalism has now, or at least recently, been posed in some other way, if it is no longer posed as the overthrow of capitalism by some other economic and political form that will come from within or without and lead to its destruction. I think this is very important, because it means (and I see that we all, each and every one of us, have a hard time thinking this through, and there are very few who risk talking about it) that perhaps we have been brought back closer to Marx, closer to the letter of Marx. For him socialism was to emerge, through the impulse of revolutionary will, out of the transformation of capitalism itself and its crises, which were tied to progress in the means of production. From this point of view, these are issues about which we might feel even more Marxist, especially about the realization of the global marketplace of which Marx spoke. It's not very original to say so, and it has been more and more often written, at least in recent years, that Marx described what he did not yet have before his eyes. One one hand, the realization of the global marketplace, even if he obviously couldn't measure the power of a fully realized globalization or what it can do (and which we now know much better); on the other, the self-transformation of capitalism through its crises. From Marx we may get the impression (although it also depends on how you read the text) that this self-transformation leads to a point of extreme fragility, to where capitalism might also be destroyed through a proper political understanding of the moment, where you can drive a lance into a machine that has become sufficiently ill. But there is also enough in Marx to see something of what can be analyzed as capitalist self-development. It is also certain that Marx poorly judged the capacity of capitalism to bounce back from its own crises. This already happened with the the great crisis of 1929 and the New Deal, and now we see capitalism since the New Deal somehow endlessly absorbing and overcoming its crises, creating others but organizing itself better and better to bounce back from them.

I have taken this whole rather long detour to say, in a manner both abusive and allusive, that if we do not take a clear, not to say revolutionary, position from which we define and denounce exploitation and propose something else, then it complicates the question a great deal, at least initially.

But in this sense it seems to me that with techno, unlike what we saw with rock music, there is no rejection of capitalism as a whole. There is simply a rejection of the complete appropriation and co-optation of festive spaces by a marketplace which tends to transform them into spectacular commodities. However, this rejection does not take place in the name of a totality of existence, so to speak, but only for this festive zone, a zone of excess, what Georges Bataille called 'expenditure.'

Yes, I think that's true; that may be what's at stake with techno, as with many other artistic behaviors, to the extent that there are no longer any grand acts or gestures of decisive refusal. One might say that in art these gestures no longer really exist. This is another time. But I think it quite interesting to try and think what a time that no longer has room for radical critique means. Radical critique no longer knows in the name of what it is to be made, since it can no longer be made in the name of another history, or another subject of history. So then there's this great suspense, where it is not forbidden to take up space or to take on form, but which obviously makes the whole thing quite fragile, or at least ephemeral, since the time when techno can really happen outside of everything else is quickly over.

Usually critics say this is nihilism, there are no more values, that is, there is no longer any difference, because saying there are no values means saying there is no difference in values. But somehow we alway have proof that this is not true. For example, techno comes along and says, this is a value; it is a value because is is not spectacle, because it's not leisure. Then, of course, this very fact, this proposition, can itself take on a commodity value. For the moment I don't see any possibility—except as a major risk, a defeat, a funeral of the first rank—of holding up as a value the counter-value of techno festiveness, because you can only do that by keeping the techno space strictly separate and secret. You fall back on being a secret society, so you have to manage to do it all clandestinely. But that necessarily goes against the very imperatives of techno, namely that anyone can come, that you have to let a certain number of people know, and so on.

That has already happened. There are now two currents in techno. On one hand, a current that is more or less separate, separated in any case, from a commercial context, organizing what they call 'free parties' or 'teknivals,' outdoors or in places they keep a secret until the last minute. And on the other hand there is the official current, where show-business professionals organize techno events the same way they used to organize rock concerts, in the same venues and costing just as much, even more. So you go from parties that are free to ones that are very expensive, and you don't get the same people at all.

That's interesting. But couldn't there a kind of growing taste for secrecy or—how to put it?—for celebrating the secret as such, or the initiation, since you have to be in on it. Which brings with it the danger of this kind of thing , namely that in a world like ours there is no initiation which does not presuppose some kind of private appropriation, fundamentally very violent, even if there is no appropriation of property. Or the risk of sanctifying something, even if it's not a person or an institution. It might well be even the very idea of the festive, the secret feast. For example, you were talking about the deep forest. But it was always the forests where secret societies met, whether brigands or Druids,

people who trafficked with fairies. This said, it is quite telling that this
split is occurring, or even, according to what you said, has already
happened within techno.

But don't raves attest to a recurrence or the resistance of the festive, of Bataille's
expenditure, as if humans needed to apportion themselves, to invent, singularly
or collectively, zones of excess?

As far as this recurrence goes, resistance *and* recurrence, one can only
say yes. They have always been, and perhaps always are, there. But what
happened after rock music, and is perhaps starting up again in more
radical fashion with techno, bears witness to impoverishment and loss on
that level, which is felt as a lack within our societies. This is undeniable,
and is surely one of the great issues for a West on the wane: how to
recover this share of expenditure. We should perhaps take a closer look
at the notion of 'recovering,' for even Bataille knew that all forms of
glory or glorious sovereignty are fallen ones (after first thinking that
they provided a solution to the question of expenditure). They correspond, as he says somewhere, to the 'gigantic failure' of all the royal and
priestly sovereignties who in the end brought only wars and misery to
the people. This is indisputable, but I would add that if the necessity of
the festive is such that it becomes a necessity for society as a whole, then
it follows that festivity occurring too far outside social space, one that
completely eludes, or tries to, society's self-representation, runs the risk
of becoming a festivity that fails in its very function. If we take the
archaic feast as a point of reference or comparison, we realize that everyone is involved, even if everyone is not a dancer. For example, not everyone may wear a mask, but on the other hand everyone is there, present,
and everyone sings (and also watches). It is difficult to determine to what
extent there is no spectacle in traditional African feasts, like those of the
Dogon, for example.

Yes, there, too, we find a contagiousness through looking, through the spectacle,
that is widely found in festivity.

That's why I have reservations about a merely critical handling of the
idea of spectacle. Not only is everyone there, but the fact that everyone is
there means that the festivities are a part of the social apparatus. But what
comes into play—and this is curious—is that when festivities become too

great a part of the social apparatus, 'we'—those who expect a truly festive element—become dissatisfied because we pick up on the commodity co-optation. But I think, in spite of everything, it also means, and this needs to be be said, that one cannot content oneself with situating the festive beyond the space of this cooptation, because then something of the representation of the festive for society will be lacking. When I say 'representation,' I mean it not in the secondary and subordinate sense, but simply that in its self- representation, say, society must have an awareness of itself as a society of festivity as well. For example, society has an awareness of itself as a society of constraint: the constraint of work, of the police, of the traffic system. And it must also have an awareness of the festive in its self-awareness. Maybe the problem is that right now society doesn't quite know how, or if, the festive fits into its self-awareness. Or that, rightly or wrongly, a part of our society likes to tell itself that it doesn't fit, that it is just 'commodity spectacle.' Indeed, there may be— and I tend to think so—another form of the festive subconscious that sustains itself another way, sometimes even in very, one might say, perverse fashion. That is, there is at least a part of our society which seems to take pleasure in or get off on the representation that our society has no festivity. This is a kind of nihilistic hyperconsumerism of nihilism itself, a way of gaily dancing on the edge of the volcano, which I think is then translated into certain artistic attitudes and positions.

From that point of view I am not ready to simply endorse an opposition between leisure and the festive if one says, for example, that all of cinema and television, and sports, too, comes under leisure. I know that a well-prepared Guy Debord-type would say, 'Of course we know very well the spectacle co-opts everything, and even operates its own critique in spectacular fashion.' Yet I wonder whether that isn't something on the order of Marx's mistaking the capacity of capitalism to get through its crises. The fact that the 'commodity spectacle' may co-opt its own opposition and in turn make it into spectacle and commodity has now reached such a level of intensity that we can say of Debord, in spite of the great difference in time, what we said of Marx. It was too soon for him to see how far it could go. It has now reached such a level intensity that there has been a change of nature, not just degree. What we call co-optation (as if we knew what could preserve some authenticity with respect to this 'co-optation) is different in nature; it is not just the recuperation by evil of something authentically good. We are not either in one regime or the other, but somewhere beyond, elsewhere, where the two things co-exist. For me it is a bit of a mystery, an enigma, but both total commodification and festivity co-exist, not total, but real.

All I mean is that there some something about the festive that seriously resists, even as it is caught in the mesh of the net. I would say as much of television, for example. It's a little different, and I'm not saying that everything on television is quality. But there is something about television that binds people to each other, contrary to what we always imagine, people sitting alone in front of the T.V. People talk about it; they talk a huge amount about what they've seen on T.V. I really think there is a collective existence to television—I don't mean the content, which is another matter. There is a real collective existence there. And for once, this existence is also the existence of a place—maybe one can't say 'festive'— but a place where there is something on the order of expenditure.

Although techno wholly tends toward this festive community, right now there is a kind of renunciation of politics, or at least of political commitment, of a stated and deliberate will to transform the social order. In that sense it is true that techno, unlike rock and rap music, is an apolitical movement. Yet to the extent that the apolitical constitutes a layer essential to, even originating or constituting our being-together, cannot one say that it is a response to another demand of that 'with' or of the political no longer based on the ideological, the utopian, or the contractual.

I notice in your question a kind of see-sawing on your part about politics, or about the use of the word 'political.' When you say 'renouncing politics, or at least political commitment' in techno, that makes it into an apolitical movement. There politics is characterized positively, in the very traditional way we always have; there is then a loss in something that is apolitical. What's more, when you say 'apolitical,' you know very well you are basically on the verge of evoking what we have always said, that what is apolitical is in fact political, that is, necessarily always reactionary. But then you immediately talk about 'the apolitical constituting a layer essential to, even originating or constituting our being-together. . . , a response to another demand of that "with" or of the political.' If we take that literally, what is striking is a kind of contra-diction, or at least an oxymoron, since you literally say that the apolitical may be essential to or constitutive of the political. If I contract the sentence, that's what I get. Except that when you say it, you say 'of that "[being-]with" or of the "political".' The equivalence indicates that you means something different by 'political' than what you meant earlier.

> *Right. It is the lack or suspension of a 'politics' constitutive of 'the political' that is at work, it seems to me, in techno festiveness, and perhaps in a number of artistic practices as well.*

It's quite compex, but I think in fact that's right. I am quite willing to admit, in that see-sawing way we have been engaging in, it is true that from one angle, at least in the terms that have now become ours, those of a certain modern tradition, there has been a disengagement from the political. But with techno I get the feeling that it takes a different form than it generally does in contemporary art. Artists, whether visual artists, film-makers, or musicians, in the main always feel close to the idea of political commitment. In recent times they are the ones who have pushed the idea forward, and they make up most visibly what we in France call 'the left of the left.' Compared to that, techno has a different look, something we would traditionally characterize as apolitical, withdrawn, uncommitted, that is, the risk of something reactive or reactionary which, because of its withdrawal and abstention, allows the dominant order (or the dominant disorder) of things to go on.

It is difficult not to at least harbor such a suspicion. But at the same time, the problem is that this makes techno no different than domesticity, let's say, to provoke techno and the people involved in it. Similarly, one could say—and I'm sure there are people of a very traditional political temperament, very militant, who do say—that it's exactly the same thing. From a political point of view it is the same thing: people who stay at home or who wrap themselves in the familial cocoon, who no longer wish to commit to anything, are doing the same thing as those who go into the forest.

> *But there is that desire, that strong will to be together.*

Yes, but a political person—it's better to call him or her an activist—could say, 'Being together, sure. But it's *you* being together, off in your little corner, but you blow off the being-together of society as such.'

> *It does seem to me that the political dimension of techno does in some sense mean a rejection of any activism, since all militant activism refers to Ideas, a*

Meaning, and a Truth that techno rejects. In any case it neither proposes nor prophecies a why or wherefore to rally around. Which doesn't mean—quite the contrary—that inside it has no concern with the present, just that it wants to be together in the present, and no longer project Meaning, Truth, and an Ideal for 'tomorrow.' 'Being together tomorrow' would be something pursuant to an Ideal still to be attained, and in the name of which one may, or may have to, sacrifice the present. This is very strong in techno.

That's interesting, but the militant may answer, 'But how do you do without tomorrow, without some project, given that the day after the techno party there will once again be social injustice, the harshness of the workplace or of unemployment? What do we do about that? And how can you do something about it if you don't do it in terms of tomorrow.' He may even say, 'O.K., I'm not talking about tomorrow in the absolute, a "radiant future," or a classless society. But I am talking about not letting Europe become something exclusively for big capital and the marketplace, and demanding from the outset the introduction of provisions for social justice in its construction.' I imagine people into techno maybe responding, 'O.K., I didn't say that when the party is over I wouldn't worry about that, too.' So, O.K.

But let's put aside this fictitious exchange, because what I think is interesting is that you see something coming that *isn't* political, not strictly, directly, or simply political. It would perhaps be better not to call it 'apolitical,' to avoid confusion. There is the apolitical as a political position, as in 'I'm apolitical.' Then there is what you said about the 'with,' a dimension of being-in-common that cannot be reduced to the political and is not equivalent to it. This is indeed something very important happening to us. A space that we might call the 'theologico-political' is very slowly closing. That is, a space into which the whole of social existence necessarily had to be almost absorbed, or in any case assumed or subsumed (allowing for, depending on the version, the carving out of certain private spheres which are themselves quite limited, inscribed in very clear fashion into the totality) in all its aspects, under the political, or more precisely, the theologico-political. That is, according to a principle of organizing meaning, a finality that in the end goes back to transcendence of the theological kind. I think the modern, contemporary world began, on this view, with Rousseau and the French Revolution, amidst a great ambivalence, a positive ambivalence that on one hand consisted of reformulating the theologico-political, and on the other of leaving it behind. It was to be reformulated in terms of the sovereign people, which soon ran into the difficulty that the people is not a god, and thus cannot be glorified in that way. Or when it is, it is pure illusion, appropriated by a party that claims to be the party of the people. There was an ambivalence between this and something quite different just coming to light (we see it in Rousseau, silently, in latent fashion, and also in Marx), the basic question, which had never before presented itself in history, namely: What is being-in-common as such, even before it is organized or ascribed to a principle? Or rather, once we no longer begin by asking according to what principle or to what end we shall organize our being-in-common, we then begin to ask ourselves what the nature of that being-in-common is. And this had already started even before Rousseau. In Hobbes, for example, we are faced with a 'state of nature' and then we ask ourselves how we can 'police' (that is, civilize, make into a *polis*, a 'city-state') that state of nature. What comes silently into view here is the fact that there is no state of nature, but there is a being-together, that is, relating—a 'with,' as you would say. It is at the origin and absolutely constitutive of existence, and has its own order of autonomy and legitimacy, one which not only cannot be reduced to the political, but, once we are past the theologico-philosophical, indeed creates its own kind of ambiguity. (This is also true of the simply theological, as we go through the experience of the 'death of God'—if one can use that expression here without its being taken as nihilist, the way it usually is—that is, in a time when a reference to transcendance cannot provide a meaning or hold things together.)

One one hand, the 'being-in-common' or the 'being-with' appears as it is, naked, but also appears in its negative form, which leads us to apprehend individuals as isolated, selfish, individualist, and atomized. That is why the whole issue of the mass and the crowd comes up—the crowd as the locus of integral atomizing, or of totalizing by compression. This question of the masses is also one of the things that makes fascism possible, in the way that it drove Freud. I really think that for the first time society appeared problematic in terms of its very bonds, whereas until then the way we controlled the bonds could be problematized. One could hold that the powers that be were bad, or the institutions, or whatever, and that on that level there might be room for change. But never had the bond been undone to the point where you had the bond on one side—the thread, if you will—and the elements to be bound on the other. Perhaps something similar had occurred with the end of the Roman Empire, but since that was more a centifugal phenemenon, and not one of globalization, it occurred through a return to small communities. Feudalism basically emerged out of those small communities. Then the state and modern society were created in a struggle against feudalism. The modern state—Louis XIV, but his predecessors, too, it should be said—took great pains to break down feudalism and to completely liquidate all the forms of local community that had had a status throughout antiquity. One could almost call them 'natural,' since for us the existence of communities and peoples seems natural. There is no doubt that the modern world comes out of the liquidation—I don't use the word critically—and the vanishing of all those forms of existence, and in the end, that of the family. This strips bare 'being-together,' 'being-with,' or 'being-in-common,' as one likes. It is no accident that the question of being-in-common is the question all of Western philosophy constantly runs into, without knowing how to ask it. We even see this in Heidegger, who holds that *Mitsein* ('being-with') is coessential with *Dasein* ('being-there'), but devotes not a single line to the meaning of *mit*, and this in an enormous tome where he is always ready to leap onto any term or concept. But he doesn't analyze it, as if everyone knew what 'with' means, whereas we have no idea of what it might mean, and there may be indeed nothing that is harder to analyze.

All that just to say I agree with what you said about the dimension of 'with,' but it also shows us there is some ambiguity between this stripping bare of the 'with' or 'together,' with dispersion and regrouping on one hand, and on the other its opposite, a 'one-world' globalization, the general standardization of conditions by an organizing power that is not a political one, in any case not theologico-political, but capitalism. And it is no accident that we hear the role of the state, or the nation, in any case, has been seriously cut into, and you now see people who used to be for the destruction of the state now calling upon it. For in the end the state seems a possible protection against being devoured by the ultra-free-market. And when there is a political crisis—and there indeed is one, but quite different from the vileness and corruption of politicians, which is only a problem because of a more fundamental collapse—it makes for a major problem, since we have no answer to it. Our only answer is in the form of a negative 'politology' or theology; that is, democracy is something that has no agency for identification, and it shouldn't have, for that creates the risk of turning back to totalitarianism. I don't think that's at all false. It may be true, but then that poses the further question of how society is to identify, because a society can't not identify itself. Curiously enough, this question of the political intersects with the question of how a society can represent to itself its own capacity for the festive.

In a sense, all your work on the notion of community (especially La Communauté désœuvrée[1] [The Idling Community] *and on being-together maintains that 'communion' is the exact opposite of community, relief in the form of a move towards fusion that means its suppression. What about 'techno-trance,' communion through the body and the dancing that seems to swirl up around it, and the 're-enchantment' it might thereby bring back to us in the present?*

You say 'techno-trance,' but isn't that an expression rejected by techno?

No. I think there is something in raves that come close to trance, through the dancing, the music, the play of the smoke machines and the lights, the movement of the crowd, the dark, the strangeness of the sites, and, perhaps, alcohol or drugs (Ecstasy or others).

I don't have much to say about trance, because I think that it has always been there in the festive. You simply need intoxication in the broad sense. Your head has to spin. There's an a old schoolboy philosopher's ditty, 'When two people dance / They go into trance. / That's what they call / Trans-cen-dance.' But when one uses the word trance, one is also referring to more than intoxication, to 'possession,' by a higher power. I can't say much here, since I don't know either the material facts of the case, or the interpretive discourse(s) of techno around this issue. One thing is certain: a trance is something on the razor's edge. And this something has a pre-eminent and pre-determined place in ritual, whether it's voodoo or any other form of mystical ecstasy. They are all very structured and involve possession by an outside demonic power. From another side, there is trance as a slide into possession by nothing, into a communal

[1] *La Communauté désœuvrée*, Ed Christian Bourgois, Paris, 1990.

fusion (just from the movement of the trance itself), or into a possession by a demonic power, which here is that of a charismatic chief.

Obviously there is no such power in techno ('Neither God nor master,' so to speak).

I agree there's no proof of anything like that for the moment, but one may wonder whether the word isn't bringing with it a taste for experiencing communing of a mystical type.

But couldn't one speak rather of ecstasy, a common ecstasy opening up as if by contagion into dancing or more generally into the global context I spoke of earlier?

Yes, but ecstasy, too, may involve a way of giving oneself over to, and passing into, an outside, a transcendence. That's what ecstasy means. I think there is a way of magnifying ecstasy, but I could also say that of Bataille, and long before that of Schelling and the ecstasy of reason. Here, too, there is an approach that risks giving way to being possessed from outside, to get 'beyond oneself,' like giving way to madness, dispossession, and so on. The core of the whole question of getting 'beyond oneself' is (or should be) a question of possession and appropriation versus dispossession or 'disappropriation.' This must be handled quite delicately, but I do mean 'disappropriation.' Just as there used to be a way of thinking of collective property as a annulment pure and simple of private property (even though what you find in Marx—and he says so explicitly in the famous 'final' chapter of *Capital*—is a distinction made between 'private property,' 'collective property,' and 'individual property'). The latter becomes a kind of third term, a dialectical 'relief,' with respect to the two others. Similarly, there ought to be a possibility in trance or ecstasy of an 'appropriation' that is both individual and collective such that a group or society itself can recognize itself in it. But by putting forth too strongly the idea or ideal of a general 'high,' you move totally into the dark.

I understand that, but I was thinking more of expenditure, or perhaps, to put it more precisely, the need to apportion out zones of expenditure in common, not just leisure spaces, but festive ones.

You just used an expression that can immediately be seen as problematic: 'apportion out expenditure.' But can expenditure be apportioned? I would agree more if we say, 'Yes, but one cannot apportion expenditure.'

Indeed, expenditure cannot be an operation or a product, but the space would at least be open, and therefore possible.

Yes, but if in fact, to put it in very formally, the conditions are present in a techno party for it to be the locus of a expenditure which, without being a calculation or reckoning (that is, it doesn't require something on the order of, 'O. K., we're going to let go at the Baths, and then we'll go to bed at *x* o'clock, because. . .'); that is, if it is really expenditure that is spent, but which creates no illusions about itself, does not think of itself as absolute or infinite, and does not seek to enter into either a total communion with the masses or a pure beyond, then what is it? You'd end up having to commit suicide; you'd have to die of an excess of dancing, alcohol, of everything—noise, light. Thus, if the conditions were there for it to be a *finite* expenditure, self-limiting in its very access to the limitless (which is the basis for all expenditure), then that would be fine. But it highlights all the more the fact that such expenditure is impossible or at least problematic. Now if we compare it to erotic expenditure—the expenditure of Bataille—we note that one of Bataille's great themes (and he says so at one point) is that erotic expenditure is only possible because it reposes on simulacrum. There Bataille imagines (a little nostalgically, perhaps) that it would obviously be better if we had access to erotic fusion. But since that is not possible, we only mimic it. So it's play-acting, and eroticism is play-acting, just as sacrifice is play-acting. Yet it is only on this condition that it is possible; otherwise it would instantly become completely destructive.

What doesn't seem quite right to me here is the somewhat reductive thinking about simulacrum, simulation, and play-acting. One can only think in those terms if one sets up a positive plenitude or primary authenticity on the erotic level that is communion-like and fusional. I fear that in the critique of the spectacle, or more generally in the simulacrum, there is an analogous logic, reposing on the ideal primacy, 'originary,' if you will, of an authentic plenitude with respect to which everything else is play-acting, simulacrum, and so on. But if it is plurality, not unity, or separation, not fusion, that is original (not 'originary' in the sense of juxtaposed solitudes, but different, too, than the coupled oppositions solitude/fusion), if it is separation that constitutes the bond (bonded

things are linked by something that is not the things themselves, and we
would not have to bond them if they weren't separate), again, if separation is constitutive and not merely a lack, then what appears to be
simulacrum isn't merely simulacrum. It is something different.

> *It also seemed to me that one could establish a surprising correspondance
> between the esthetics of mixing (of a multiplicity of different musical identities)
> in techno and the real 'mixing' of ethnic and national identities [as in the French
> and Canadian* métis *and Hispanic* mestizo*], especially as they are both possible
> only with the present-day development of new technologies. Can't one
> conclude that what we have here is a convergence of art and technics into a
> force for deterritorialization and thus for* métissage *?*

The question of mixing and *métissage*. . .

> *To the extent that that mix is made possible by new technologies like samplers,
> which allow you to articulate all sorts of musical identities, to hybridize them
> into a* métissage*. . .*

I do think, without going so far as to laud *métissage* the way Michel
Serres did, trying with good will but a little naively to pre-empt an issue
that was precisely the most tense one, that *métissage* and mixing are a
fundamental, one might even say permanent, condition for all
constituting. How did sexual reproduction come about? It is easy to see,
and any biologist will tell you so, that sexual reproduction at the very
least, even without according it any finality, represents the possibility of
overcoming a certain monotonous repetition of the individual that non-
sexual reproduction involves. This is already 'mixing.' All forms of
organization derive from mixing and *métissage*. And at bottom, pure
things are never anything but extracted. Pure gold, pure water, not to
mention pure race, are nothing but extracts, artificial fabrications.
Indeed, one of the main features of modern technics is precisely that it
introduced a number of new forms of mixing and *métissage*, between the
visual and sound, between drawing and color, between the plane and
depth, as well as between different sonorities. And after all, this is
nothing more than the repetition of all the forms of mixing and *mélange*
that have always presided over the constitution of new moments, and of
cultural or national entities.

Don't these new technologies make this all the more manifest and accelerate the movement of métissage? *By multiplying communications networks all over the planet, don't they engage in a process of deterritorialization, and therefore of* métissage?

Yes, only I wonder whether under *métissage* or mixing in general, we're not including two very different things. One is putting together two forms that start out as heterogeneous or foreign to each other, something like collage. This attests more to the degree of insecurity or instability of the forms in question, as when the Mona Lisa, by virtue of its age as a form, begins to have a certain history, so Duchamp can sticks a mustache on her, even if this is not quite a true 'mixing,' because it's a parody.

But in techno, mixing is something else, not just collaging two musical identities together. To put it succinctly, it is the production of something new through a diversity or heterogeneity of different musical or acoustic identities.

Yes, but that's something I probably fail to appreciate because of my lack of familiarity with it. Another thing *métissage* might be is the constitution of a new form. This is something I want us to be more attentive to. There has been such an enthusiasm about *métissage* and multiculturalism that it has become particularly necessary and urgent, because of the horrible Bosnian affair, and other less horrible but no less urgent affairs in a country like ours, to stand up for the necessity of cultures to cohabit, to encounter each other. It is no less certain, I think, that a simple coexistence, mélange or collage, will not suffice, and that at some point, new forms must be produced. That can take a very, very long time, just as the various Romance languages, French, Spanish, Romanian, Italian, were the product of a series of processes, the decomposition of Latin and the recomposition by mixing with other languages, which took centuries. But new forms did appear. . . What I mean is that the question of form is a real one, as is the question of a work. Not out of a taste for forms—'We must have a new form'—but because despite everything, form, as we might say in the Nietzschean style, is also what protects us against the abyss of *fond,* the 'ground' or depths, 'the bottomlessly profound.' One might also say that form is precisely the means through which the abyss presents itself.

In your most recent texts, especially Une pensée finie (A Finite Thinking), Être singulier pluriel (Being Singular Plural), Corpus, Le poids d'une pensée (The

Weight of a Thought), *and* Les Muses, *'the question of technics' is always disussed in relation to what you call elsewhere 'the withdrawal of appropriable meaning,' that horizon of finitude that nothing—no meaning, given or produced, divine or ideological—can henceforth ever fulfil. Are you saying that only art and technics, what the Greeks called* techné), *'of which 'art' is only ever a translation,' as you said in* Les Muses, *can designate our manner of being and sharing existence in this world, which no longer admits of being thought or dwelt in terms of the figure of Meaning, Ideas, or Ideologies?*

Indeed. I am ready to state that the greatest task facing us now is the task of thinking something as meaning in the absence of any given, recognizable or appropriable meaning. When you say 'withdrawal of appropriable meaning,' that's one way of saying it. Elsewhere you also spoke of 'an absence of meaning' (Bataille), 'open meaning' (Adorno), 'problematic meaning' (Patocka), as well as of 'absent meaning' (Blanchot).

First, of all these expressions I prefer Blanchot's 'absent meaning' (as I think you do, too), but I don't mean it's the only one. We of course understand that it is not an 'absence of meaning,' but a meaning that takes on meaning in its absence—one might even say, since its absence. This is something I think art is now in fact reaching toward, and has been for a long time now. It has been doing so insistently, with an insistance that may at times be overheated, excessive or disordered. But the point of its insistence is correct, that for the moment meaning no longer gives of itself—it cannot—but this moment is not some small passing moment of our choosing, but a complete transformation of things, equivalent to the one by which the West came about. I really think the West is coming apart, being dethroned because it has become equivalent to the whole world. Westernization is now over. Well, there's the Westernization of the globe, and then there's the globalization of the West. And what's certain is that this transformation occurs through the absence, or rather absenting, of figures like meaning, and therefore of ideas and ideologies. From this point of view, what is at stake in what we have been calling 'the end of ideology' is of capital importance. And this must somehow be related to the fact that after rock music something like techno comes along, where you don't even have anything that constitutes a new ideology. At least rock could claim an ideology of peace and love, one that could in any case designate its ideological enemies a lot more clearly. It's important, provided we don't, with the last energy we have, sidestep the question thus posed. It's not what some have called the end of ideology—'Great! It's over; there's no more ideology.'—where with a wave of the hand we find ourselves, as night follows day, under an ideology of ultra-individualism because there is nothing else to take the place of what has been swept away. This now empty terrain is not empty at all, for it is the ground that gives rise to meaning, and with great urgency. I think it important, if only as a preliminary approach to the question, to remember that when meaning was presented using great figures—God, the nation, the state—when totalitarianisms were being formed, rather than the will to presentation of meaning there was more of an immediate absorption of it. And even before that, meaning, as presented or figurative, was never a fulfilled or saturated, as we all too easily believe. The experience of meaning has, I believe, always been the experience of a relationship to something impossible, infinite, or unfathomable. I like to say that true Christians never died in the sweet blessedness of their happiness at going to Heaven. First of all, they could never die knowing that they were among the Elect, because one can never know that one is among the Elect; anyone who claims to is not among the Elect. This also came up, of course, in the nineteenth-century critique of religion as an opium of the people, their consolation. (This is not to deny all that can be said against the Church—Protestantism, too, by the way. Nor is there any reason, in passing, to spare Islam and Judaism.) But that said, the role of religious institutions and powers is one thing, and the experience that takes place there is quite another. By that I mean that we could approach it all quite differently if, instead of thinking, 'Oh, what a catastrophe! Suddenly we've managed to lose all meaning,' we were to remind ourselves that the most acute consciousness of meaning may always have been that of its absence, though expressed through other modalities. And indeed, perhaps the awareness we spoke of a moment ago—the awareness of the limits of the festive, and thus of the incompleteness of what the festive seems to offer, fusion, ecstasy, etc.—is precisely our consciousness of the non-presence of being. I believe this can be taken quite far, if only to make one small point, a rather cold theoretical or conceptual one. Meaning either means referring to something else, with respect to which it has meaning; or, it necessarily means the relation of one to the other, for there is no meaning for something isolated (as Bataille said, 'There is meaning only severally.') Or else, in a third meaning of the word 'meaning, sense,' as in 'sense of

direction,' it all comes together. All at once meaning lies in this opening
to the other, but if the other is absorbed or identified, then it no longer
has meaning.

> *In* Les Muses[2] *you bring up the fact that 'many of today's artworks, perhaps far
> too many, are in the end only their own theory,' justifying it somehow by what
> you call that 'deaf need driving artists. . .to present "art" itself.'[3] You seem to say
> we must go beyond the 'pure act of presentation enclosed in itself,'[4] to set aside
> the autonomy of art for art's sake. But what could the task of art be, if not the
> presentation either of the Idea or of art itself'?*

It's obvious that what is most certainly at stake in art today is art
itself, its nature, status and meaning—even its role. This is nothing new;
it's something which began with Hegel and continued through
Duchamp. Here it is important to stress that what many have said over
the last few years—that philosophy has taken over art in some totally
illegitimate way, forcing it to tell all kinds of metaphysical tales it has no
business doing—is not at all the case. Quite the contrary; these are most
fundamental questions for the modern world and its civilization, which
have cast art into a privileged but risky role: not of having it tell us
things, but rather of posing the question of the very modes in which
meaning is to be presented. As soon as meaning is no longer set down in
identifiable instances, one can no longer have an art that corresponds to
it. First, there can no longer be a religious art; secondly, there can no
longer even be figurative art, because even the face or form of things can
no longer be the site of an appearance or manifestation of meaning. By
the same token, it may even be that art becomes problematic, at least to
the extent that it designates a certain order of activity, at bottom of
specific techniques—specified, too, by a certain finality, whether the
beautiful, the sublime, or the two together, conceived as services to the
divine, or to glory in general (here again from the theologico-political
point of view). Nor is it surprising that as it has become problematic, the
notion of art has at the same time exposed itself to having its own
problems being worked by artists themselves, if only when they ask,
'Where does art stand?' This is what Duchamp had already undertook in
various guises.

[2] Ibid p.147
[3] Ibid, p.157
[4] Ibid, p.147

It is not surprising that at the same time the most primitive substratum of the word 'art' was brought to light, that is, '*technique*.' Contrary to what one might have thought, it was not machines that came to replace painting or written music, but the the general technicity of man, destined to supplement nature, which for Aristotle was the definition of art: art executes the way nature does, that is, proceeding in relation to an end, but it executes that which nature does not. It is a great curse, and paradox, that under the words 'technique,' technics, Greek *techné*), we first of all mean the underlying mechanics of something, the machinery or instrument, then secondly, some kind of monstrous autonomous power we are unable to grasp. Whereas technics is us, in the constant execution of our humanness, especially since the Neolithic. Since then we have transformed, supplemented, and indeed partly destroyed nature. Thus today there is a singular conjuction of art and technics—technics stripping art of its 'estheticity' and sacredness, as well as its characteristic gratuitous and decorative beauty, one the one hand, and on the other, an appeal, either a call, a question, or a concern, on the part of art to technics: how to provide something of the orderliness of meaning, but a meaning open to the fact of its own absence (what in fact art had always provided). The result is a technics I like to define as the operation of means toward an end that is not given. This is basically the same thing Aristotle was saying: Nature is what operates means, in and of itself, towards a end given by nature itself. The flower grows to become a flower. What disqualifies this model for us, the flower and 'the rose that grows without reason,' is that the reason for the rose *is* the rose, while we don't know what the reason for our technics is, because we don't have the rose, that is, a finality. It was long thought that on the whole technics was moving toward both science and happiness—happiness as health or comfort, for example, or as mastery and ownership of nature, as Descartes had it. But it is very striking how much technics has now stripped and bared itself as not having ends. So we are no longer at all sure that it will provide happiness, and it it becomes impossible to detach from it some entity like 'science' as absolute knowledge. But this also means rethinking ourselves as ends, as Kant said, not as beings that relate to and through given ends, but as beings having to incessantly initiate, rediscover, or rather invent their finality.

While a number of critics and art historians complain about the 'non-sense' and insignificance of contemporary art, regretting the loss of the One, of Beauty, and the Ideal, don't you think that on the other hand, the arts now tend to fragment and fracture the One, Meaning or Truth, opening them up to a multiplicity of voices and paths, prospectives and perspectives for an art and existence on the basis and ground of inappropriable meaning? And that this may be both art's task and its destiny?

I don't think that art 'tends to fragment the One' or however you put it. In one sense I could say that art does nothing; it doesn't take the initiative (but neither does philosophy). It resonates with something that is happening, and notes passages in, and of, history. I say this, first of all, to avoid a manner of speaking that invokes intention or will (good or ill), as if we decided one day to 'fragment,' the next to 'unify,' another to invent perspective, and yet another to do performances. Let's take for a moment the expression that art 'realizes,' in the sense of 'renders, ' something. Thus art was once a realization of the Greek city-state, then of the world of Christianity, and so on. In this it does no more than other cultural forms or formations, but it does so in accordance with its property as 'art.' What is that property? One may attempt an answer to this question by saying that this 'property' of 'art' first became manifest for us precisely at the moment when art was stripped or bared of its theologico-political functions—with the advent of our contemporary world. That was also the advent of a shaking of foundations, the basic units, ideals, absolutes, or whatever we call them. What happened then— let's say between Kant and Romanticism, between Mozart and Beethoven, between Chardin and Fuseli—'promoted' art, so to speak, to an autonomous and separate function formerly hidden amongst the theologico-political offices it held. That function was to record (inscribe, resonate, present) the dissipation, even disappeance, of the great forms which granted access to the 'ground' (to meaning or truth, as one prefers).

And therefore also the function (if one can call it a function!) of noting the stripping and flaying of that 'ground' or its absence (its withdrawal or absenting itself). Or even the impossibility of grasping it as ground—indeed, the need to encounter it as abyss, flight, shattering, fragmentation, fracture, and so on. Now dissonance sounds where once there was nothing but consonance, harmony, and counterpoint. We began to call the echo of that dissonance 'art' (for this meaning of the word barely existed, if at all), because it is neither religious, nor scientific, nor political. (In this sense, 'art' now denotes the outlines of a new religion, although an unknown one.) This doubtless means in a more general way that, just as it did before the modern world, art has to deal with that which not organizable by religion, knowledge, or power. And maybe with that which is not organizable at all, unpresentable.

What do you think of the ongoing debate about contemporary art, the polemic or 'quarrel', whether art today is in crisis, whether there has been a 'failure' of representation, or even worse, as Baudrillard declares, an 'art conspiracy.' All these complaints derive from the painful judgment of the impossibility, or rather incapacity, of contemporary art to provide meaning.

The whole debate around contemporary art and its 'crisis' seems to me burdened, very heavily so, by a failure to recognize that 'art' in still in childbirth. (I mean the modern birth spoken of above; one can also discuss its birth in the absolute sense.) It is both a witness to the crisis and itself in crisis. Just think of what separates the realm of art in 1750 from the same realm in 1850, above all the fact that in that hundred-year interval 'art' itself appeared, with its concept or concepts, its requirements, expectations, and problems. (And over and above that, to thicken the plot, the 'artist' also appeared.)

I therefore find it simply stupefying that the whole debate—sometimes in both camps simultaneously—seems to presume we already know what 'art' is. Nothing is less certain! When Hegel famously said that art 'is and remains for us a thing of the past,' by art he meant everything that had been meant until then by 'art' or the 'fine arts': a mode of presenting or representing something of truth (meaning), a way that could be arranged in parallel and into a hierarchy with other modes (religion, politics, science, philosophy). But Hegel could not guess how much what he was describing was also the opening up of 'art' into its modern position, at once stripped bare and exposed to enormous risks: a 'neither this nor that' which had doubtless never explicitly shown itself before in history.

Of course there is a crisis. I would even say, and not just to be provocative, so much the better. According to Poussin, Caravaggio was already 'destroying painting,' and don't even mention Manet! Of course this means many failures and much waste, waywardness and insignificance.

(There were people at the time who had no better use for the revelatory but still-new perspective than to revel in its *trompe-l'œil*.) But it also means risks, and therefore chances. It means even more: that already, though it doesn't allow us to divine much about it, here or there an artistic act or gesture rips away for us something of a future that is by its very essence a stealthy one.

> *Just like the DJ in techno—because what he proposes is not a work, but an event or experience to be lived, a context to dwell in or share, to the point where it is not his mix that makes up the work, but the rave itself—for the last ten years or so we have seen more and more attempts in contemporary art to create not artworks or objects, but processes, contexts or situations to be experienced and experimented with in common. What do you think the replacement of a representational logic by a participatory one means for contemporary art? Should we see at work here a need or demand to involve spectators in the experience of the artwork, no longer keeping them isolated and separated from the creative process but making it into a political experience, an experience of the 'with'?*

Frankly, I still have great reservations about this issue. On one hand, 'participation' covers many ambiguities: there's contagion, collective delirium, group hysteria, the misguided parades in Nuremberg and in Eisenstein's *The General Line* (whether sincere or not). On the other, one cannot simply divide it down the line, with participation on one side and representation on the other. The art of representation has certainly brought in participation. Conversely, a desire for participation can bring about its own representation in the most artificial sense of the term. At the risk of shocking you, I admit that when I'm at a party I sometimes wonder whether it isn't the mise-en-scène of festivity.

Here I would like to raise a more general problem worth discussing with respect to some of the questions you have been asking (and some that I have been asking myself, that we all ask ourselves). This is the question of the mode or regime we use for the analysis and interpretation of certain phenomena. If people go off somewhere in the forest to get together and dance to sampled or mixed music, may I thereby infer, by some literal transcription, that they are outside the theologico-political order and the received canon, outside 'unity' and 'imposed meaning'? It's not that obvious! There's also a rather dubious tendency to privilege interpretation: I do a performance, and I state that this performance means such-and-such. (I have on occasion read declarations of meaning for performances, for example, by Beuys, if memory doesn't deceive, that were real user's manuals.) Furthermore, the performance is meant to be significant as a performance because the performance as such means such-and-such.

I might add that no doubt we should distinguish between something that is a social phenomenon waiting for an analysis (a type of festivity, for example) and something that in some way presents itself as the production of a 'work' (or even a performance). They are not at all the same thing, but two very different registers of experience, even though they may communicate. I am a little uncomfortable extrapolating from techno to art or vice-versa.

Furthermore, doesn't the sovereign and brilliant subjectivity of the artist necessarily extend the world of bourgeois individualism and its ideology of commodity spectacle? In Une Pensée finie (Finite Thinking) *you imply that the necessary critique of simulation and the simulacrum can—and has—only come about against the ground of a metaphysics of the subject, which presupposes the proper or correct use of representation and appropriation. Yet one cannot deny that—as we are already starting to see with techno, to the extent that its present institutionalization tends to anesthetize and neutralize it—society lives by absorbing its marginals, transforming everything into spectacle. How does one maintain the necessary resistance to the spectacular and at the same time avoid extending a metaphysics of the subject, and with it the possibility of a proper self-appropriation.*

I would add the following. The constant movement through which the 'spectacle' does indeed absorb and resorb its own 'edges' and marginals (and its critique, too, of course: all you have to do is look at the present-day consumption of Situationism on the intellectual and journalistic scene) is also the movement through which other 'edges' endlessly form (and deform). As is attested by what you yourself told me about the evolution and transformation of techno. It is a kind of expanding universe that endlessly folds and unfolds new edges and extremities. In one sense, of course, one could say that it all cancels itself out in commodity-spectacular monotony. In another sense, why don't we just say everything is made more acute in the impossibility of holding to received oppositions—authentic vs. alienated, original vs. simulacrum, inventive vs. repetitive? The entire fabric unravels in our fingers, and we have no higher point of view from which to judge the value and significance of what is happening. This doesn't mean it's all a matter of indifference, but that only a closer look at this unraveling allows us to detect a few threads in the process of forming new knots.

Note: I have re-read the transcript of this interview, which turns out to be problematic, even unfaithful, because of problems with the tape recorder. In an attempt to respect the totality of the data, I have made only slight corrections where necessary or helpful for comprehension, and have avoided any 're-writing.'—Jean-Luc Nancy

An Interview with Michel Maffesoli

It is apparent there are innovative aspects to techno, especially its esthetics, 'mixing,' its relationship to new technologies, and its lack of a political position. Yet it remains marked by behaviors that originate in the festive and in what Georges Bataille called 'expenditure.' Couldn't one say the impact of this phenomenon may be explained by the fact that these behaviors have somehow been emptied of their substance, anesthesized or transformed into leisure and 'spectacular commodity,' at least within the Western horizon-line of economic laissez-faire individualism? *In other wars, has techno revived or reactivated the latter by bringing back to the festive its power to bind and share?*

There are two different things here: one one hand, has it been co-opted, and on the other, is there, all the same, still a dimension of authenticity to the festive? I pay much more attention to the second aspect, to the fact that there is something in techno that connects to this idea of expenditure. Of course, this is not expenditure in the pure state, the way Bataille observed it in the societies he was analyzing, but I do not believe pure states exist. To put it differently, there is the persistence of an archetype of expenditure, and then there are the modulations it undergoes as it is expressed at vatious moments. Techno may be one of the contemporary modulations, what I would call the 'postmodern' modulation, of Bataille's notion of expenditure. In this sense it reactivates, in the strong sense of the word, the festive, that desire to lose oneself in, or even to fuse with, the other, as well as the power of the festive to transfix the individual body.

It is nonetheless true that there may be, over all those the terms you are using, something on the order of co-optation going on, something causing it all in fact to be integrated into a system, whether commerce or spectacle. I don't pay much attention to it, or to be precise, I think it exists, it's a fact, but in many respects, it's marginal. One always observes some co-optation, but the 'wish to live,' so to speak, displaces or overcomes it somewhat. You'd have to go back and see whether in societies where the festive emerged there wasn't also co-optations of the commercial type or, if they couldn't express themselves within the terms of economic *laissez-faire*, found other means of imposition and constraint. As you see, I think we all too often tend to see only the constraint and alienation side of it, and thus forget the dimension of excess that tends to express itself on the edges.

> *If in the trances it provokes at its parties, as if by contagion, techno evokes something of the possession dances of traditional societes (West African voodoo ceremonies or Siberian shamanic dancing, for example), we should also add that it only preserves the outer form, or envelope, of the sacred, that which actually takes possession of man. If it is a continuation of the latter, it is only in secularized, 'desacralized' form. Does this not prove that the sacred, with its mythological and divine figures may disappear, although leaving its imprint or trace, that is, the demand for self-transcendance and transgression it implies?*

I'm always afraid when I say (thinking of what I said earlier), 'There used to be this, and now it's no more.' It's always back to the old days, a nostalgia for the Golden Age, 'It was better back then,' in every domain—we are all too used to analyzing things in this way. Actually, I would say that here we are confronted with a contemporary form of the sacred, even though strictly speaking it is not the sacred as we see it in shamanism or possession, nor in the way we will now analyze it after the fact. But at the very least, from a heuristic point of view, wouldn't it be useful, with respect to this excess and transgression, to see in it something like what I call 'the contemporary modulation of the sacred'? I say that because those whose experience these trance phenomena do so with great intensity. I see no reason to question their intensity, nor even their authenticity.

Of course, I can exercise my critical spirit and, as I did earlier, bring up the fact that they take place within an economic context. Yet—and this is what interests me in the end—the people are always invested in the moment itself. And at that moment, in many respects they are not concerned about how it is being co-opted. I would rather stress the forms of intensity and, in the most simple sense of the word, the 'investment' on the part of the actors, one which bears all the hallmarks of authenticity. We don't need to practice the theory of suspicion here. We are always looking for something else behind what we are given to see or experience, but I see no reason for suspecting those who truly practice those moments of excess and transgression.

Far from questioning this intensity, I would, on the contrary, ask whether the exhaustion or withdrawal of the 'fully sacred', in the sense of a sacred grounded in the religious and the mythological, does not also open up into something else, a sacred that is 'empty,' so to speak, without gods or other sacred figures, but where that intensity nonetheless continues to be experienced and shared, as if, in the end the sacred were the intensity itself.

For those who experience it, it is 'full.' It is, after all, a 'true' sacred, and one cannot measure the sacred of today by the standard of the sacred of another time, because it doesn't lend itself to comparison. For we only know it through an effort of erudition that certainly may have its uses, but does not allow us to say it no longer exists.

The sacred is, in a strict sense, that which allows one to go beyond oneself. It is something on the order of ecstasy. Although you haven't mentioned it, it's no coincidence that one of the main ingredients of techno is called Ecstasy. One may think what one wants, but that form of ecstasy also exists, and I see no reason why mystical or religious ecstasy, as we see it in Christianity, for example, should be considered more legitimate than the kind we see today.

In your last book Du Nomadisme: Vagabondismes initiatiques[1], *you note that here has never been as much circulation as now, 'when the technostructure thought it had everything fixed in place, ordered and foreseen.' How does one think through this paradox, where there seems to be an alliance or convergence between techno, the trance, and the technological, whereas technics seems to be set up essentially to dam, channel, or even suppress the overflow of any communion or ecstasy? And wouldn't the primary consequence of any such 'alliance' be to deterritorialize 'being-together,' thereby moving toward métissage and nomadism?*

[1] in Le Livre de Poche, Paris, 1997

We should note that human or social forms are not necessarily un-touchable, and if at a certain point, in the nineteenth century, technics had the function you described, there is nothing to show that it still does. Just as Hegel spoke of a 'ruse of History,' we can speak of a 'ruse of technics' or of a 'ruse of the imaginary.'

There is something that causes technics not to isolate itself; it tends, rather, to re-enchant the world. One can show how the Internet, the video-clip, and the use of technics in those huge techno assemblies, the raves, favor this re-enchantment. During a period of outrageous domi-nation of nature, technics was the vector of a generalized rationalization, as we see in Max Weber; at other moments there can be an inversion of phase or polarity. I think we can even see the outlines of such an inversion in what Martin Heidegger called the 'turn.' After his book on 'the question of technics,' he was able to show how in a 'relativist' perspective technics might be the key element of a more global, holistic perspective on the human. He had some intuition of this, an intuition it would befit us to pursue. I would pursue it by noting that at present it happens that, empirically and quite concretely, that technics favors a form of sacralization, of communion, and therefore of religiosity, something on the order of *reliance*, a term proposed by Bolle de Bal. He uses it in a general sense, but with technics, I would take it all the way. In those great festive gatherings, in particular, technics serves as an aid to a form of fusion, even confusion.

Thus, one can no longer simply stigmatize technics. Besides the musical example we are discussing, there is also the example of the Internet, which in addition to an obvious functional dimension there is no point in denying, there is also a sacred dimension, *reliance* as 're-liaison, re-linking,' and it is important to take this into consideration.

Couldn't one say that this change or transformation of technics as a force for liaison and communion was in the end only made possible because technics itself changed as it went from an age of mechanical industry to the present-day electronic or digital age, no longer based on a machine-like state apparatus, but on machines like computers and samplers that anyone can appropriate?

Yes, it's true there is something on the order of re-appropriation, which was not the case when the only technics possible was a state monopoly. Just think of television in Europe, for example, when they could come up with one or two kinds of soup good for everybody when there were only one or two channels. This analysis no longer applies, if only because now there is a multiplicity, and potentially an even greater multiplicity, of channels. Consequently a kind of fractalization of that technics has occurred. So, yes, I think there is re-appropriation, and here computers are interesting, since, as many researchers have shown, they have a strong element of play, the ludic element. And that is one of the characteristics of postmodernity. When we ask where post-modernity comes from, we are first referred to what has been called architectural post-modernism. It, too, was something that attempted to go beyond simple technical functionality (in this field, that of the Bauhaus and Le Corbusier). To my mind on can easily bring this notion of architectural post-modernism into the relativist perspective peculiar to the present-day fragmentation of technics. This diffraction of technics affords anyone the possibility of co-opting it, with the proviso, of course, that he or she appropriate it. And it is here that the ludic reappropriation begins. This has not often been analyzed in France, but my Canadian colleagues, in particular, have effectively brought out this dimension, even something as simple as the club, as in the games clubs that started around the use of that computer software.

You have already brought up this ludic dimension back when people began using the telephone-based Minitel data system in France.

That's true, although there's no point even talking about it now that it's over. By the way, the Minitel got its start with Gretel, and wasn't destined for the kind of use it later had. But there quickly occurred a kind of *détournement* or 'diversion' Situationist-style of Gretel, which was originally something quite technical and functional. The functionality continued to exist, but the technics, given the Situationist tactic of *détournement*, even though it wasn't thought of that way, had changed.

It also seems to me that the Internet has also been 'taken over' from its primary function, which was military.

Indeed. As you know, it was meant for wartime, to allow computer connectivity to survive.

When you assert that today 'images are plural' and that 'there are as many meanings of image as there are groups,'[2] aren't you also saying that this 'plurality' affects Meaning as being what links us, and that this link, this 'being-together,' may also be fragmented or disseminated, whence the phenomenon of 'tribalization' whose impact you have demonstrated elsewhere[3]? In other words, doesn't this fragmentation of meaning and of the collective come from the 'withdrawal' of Truth, God, and the Ideal, that is, from the impossibility in which we find ourselves, at least in the West, of figuring and structuring the world, being-in-the-world and being-together into some kind of Unity?

I think this is an intuition we should of course develop, for it would allow us to ground the link which exists between the re-emergence of the image and polytheism. Monotheism in the strict sense, whether Judeo-Christian or political, as in the Marxian or Marxist tradition, tends to deny the image in the name of reason, whether the reason of the Christian God, the whole of Western rationalism, or specifically the reason at the origin of the scientific development of the technostructure. Whereas a proliferation of images is related more to a multiplicity of lesser values.

I am struck by the connection to a period that interests me a great deal, the second and third century of our era. Peter Brown, a historian at Berkeley, has shown that during that period, just before Christianity became the Catholic Church, there was a kind of proliferation of lesser images within Christianity, which was also considered one of the mystery religions of the moment. He uses an expression which I find interesting: this was a period of 'little talking gods.' Around each image, whether that of a bishop, or the tomb of a saint, or a particular mystery cult (of which a great variety came and went) aggregations formed around a totem. Each time the image returns, we see a form of these small aggregations emerge around the image. One can also cite the sociologist Émile Durkheim and what he called 'the emblematic function of the image,' of which the totem was one of the manifestations or expressions. In my opinion something on this order is once again coming into play. That is, whatever the image, aggregations will form, in keeping with the cultural or cultic tastes of our time.

[2] Michel Maffesoli, « Des utopies interstitielles », interview with Jérôme Sans, in Blocnotes, n°4, autumn 1993, p.43
[3] Michel Maffesoli, *Le temps des tribus, le déclin de l'individualisme dans les sociétés de masse*, le Livre de Poche, coll. Biblio essais, Paris, 1988

Wouldn't that relate to what some have called 'the end of ideology' or the exhaustion of 'one-way' meaning?

I myself don't like the expression 'end of ideology' at all. There is no 'end of ideology'; there is ideological bricolage. Of course, there is no one ideology that has meaning and finality. But there are lesser ideologies, where meaning lives on in the act. What has ended is thinking that only that which had one meaning had any meaning, only that which was oriented somewhere. Quite obviously, this meaning is no more. There is no ideology that provides Meaning, whether it be Marxism, functionalism, or even Freudianism.

On the other hand, there is a multiplicity of lesser stories or histories, lesser ideologies, and lesser images that I share with others and which exhaust themselves in the act. And here we come back to the idea of intensity, of the 'present.' This 'present' implies there isn't necessarily anything on the order of extension: we do not tend *toward* something, but are tended *in*. Here I oppose *ex-tend* and *in-tend*, in the sense that I am 'tended' [or 'tense'] with others in the present. Once again we come back to the idea of expenditure. We no longer tend toward some ideal, but together we lose ourselves in the moment. This is an ancient notion that we first find in pre-Socratic philosophy, the idea of *kairos*, 'the right moment.' In a more trivial sense, it connotes 'good timing' or opportunity. It is also something we find—and this is of no small import—in the most eastern aspect of Greek philosophy. This is the idea, found in Eastern philosophy but absent from that vast movement become ours in the West, Judeo-Christianity, that there is neither beginning nor end. Everything is perpetual beginning. (This is also the great Dionysian theme.)

As the theologico-political exhausts itself or becomes obsolete, does art, in its broader primary sense, going back to the techné *of the Greeks, which includes both technics and popular arts, and of which techno might be a contemporary figure, then become the privileged site for the production of the 'images' around which the multiple and heterogeneous forms of being-together gather, if only in ephemeral fashion?*

Yes. Even though it is now a commonplace heard in various contexts, we do tend much more to make our lives into a work of art, without quite making life into a work of art. I do think there is something like this happening, in more or less diffuse fashion, verbalized or not, and it

goes to what I call the qualitative aspect of existence. It is, in sum, a
response of the collective unconscious, which no longer puts faith in
work as the only path to self-realization, or to the realization of the
world. Or rather (and this goes back to what I just said about life as a
work of art), we no longer want creativity to be reduced to work. In fact,
creativity is a constant; each of us creates. At some point, this dimension
of creating was reduced in our work lives, and work being an imperative,
creativity, too, was thereby reduced. It seems to me that at present this
reduction is growing. So we go back to creating, in the same way we said
techné was a force of linking, liaison, and 'reliance.' Technics may indeed
be at the origin of effervescent expressions like those great festive and all-
consuming, not consumerist, gatherings of today. These great gatherings
are the expression of that need, still unconscious to itself, to give existence
a qualitative meaning.

This somehow recalls condensations of energy, as in the image of the
black hole in astrophysics. But when I talk to politicians, the deciders, I
realize they never quite manage to understand these forms of conden-
sation, simply because these contemporary forms of being-together are
not being projected. And indeed, these condensations cannot be seized
with the instrumentation we have, which is still that of the 'project.' I
still maintain that many of the youthful practices occurring in these great
festive gatherings are practices of true intensity, where there are forms of
solidarity, generosity, or, going back to what I said before, true forms of a
qualitative sharing of existence.

> *Just like with the techno D.J., someone who proposes not a work, but an event
> to be lived, a context to dwell in. It's not his mix that makes the work, but the
> rave itself, the dancing community at play there. In contemporary art, we see
> more and more attempts to create not artworks, not even objects, but contexts
> or situations to be experienced and experimented with in common. What need
> does this demand to replace the logic of 'representation' with the logic of
> 'participation' come from? Are we seeing an emergence of the need to involve
> the spectator in the creative experience, to somehow make it into a 'political'
> experience, an experience of 'with'?*

I'd like to pick up on a word you used—the idea of 'representation.'
It seems to me there has been a kind of implosion of representation. The
first to show this was Jean-François Lyotard. Corresponding to that

implosion of philosophical representation, we are now also seeing an implosion of political representation. Here there is something on the order of disaffection, in the most simple sense of the word. There is a growing lack of interest in politics or in labor causes. This torments politicians and, quite rightly, drives them crazy.

But alongside representation comes the 'presentation' of things. What is presentation? It is presenting not the event, but the advent, of things. We can see quite concretely how, in a gathering, we present ourselves and what is going on around us, with no projection. I think there is good reason to reflect on this slippage from representation to presentation. I maintain that all the paroxysmal forms like great musical gatherings are manifestly of this type.

In another domain, the slippage of the political towards what I call the 'domestic' may also be a kind of presentation, here not life tending toward a future, but an investment in the present. The point is always to direct life, but not directed by a conception of society as pyramid, or by a distant realization to come. One again, the crazed rush into the distant, the radiant future, these 'hinter-worlds,' as Nietzsche would call them, has not rid us of that need for intensity which drives us to melt into the moment, into the present. We do it in slightly animal fashion almost: to live here because we are here. We are present, and present what exists.

Doesn't the term 'pyramid' you just used imply the idea of a verticality in social relationships, to which one could oppose 'participation' as a horizontal mode of relating?

In representation there is something on the order of projection. We need to look at how classicism and the classical were something that has been called the optical style. It has been opposed to—and I will come back to the idea of 'participation'—the baroque, with the idea that the classical is 'optic,' while the baroque is 'haptic,' from the Greek *haptos*, 'touch.' Is is applied to the Baroque, of course, because all the various elements of it interpenetrate and correspond, thus going back to an idea of 'magic participation.'

Throughout human history we have always been concerned with one question: How does it hold? To put it simply, glue. The alchemists of the Middle Ages, wondering what made it hold, spoke of the *glutinum mundi*. Let's think about this *glutinum*, this 'glue of the world.' On can easily imagine how, at a certain moment, the glue became 'the democratic ideal,' as Hannah Arendt saw it, the distant perspective of politics. At certain other moments, this 'world glue' is that which acts as a glue on the very moment itself, on the present. This is what happens in the fusion, or rather confusion, of the great musical gatherings, where we stick starting with the sweat of the other. One of my researchers, who works on funk and other forms of contemporary music—funk also means 'sweat,' I believe—has shown how the search for the sister soul no longer takes place at a distance, but but by sticking to the other. This is a metaphor one can apply to what we are discussing here: there are moments when the glue is created in the act itself.

Thus the pyramid is verticality; the tactile dimension is touching, horizontality. Here I think there is something on the order of a short-circuit, 'immanent transcendence.' Verticality, that which is transcendent, is God, representation, politics, and the state—something overbearing. While in those great 'haptic' gatherings there is, in various ways, in their contemporary viscosity, something that extends beyond the individual and falls onto the group. That's the image I'd like to get across, although it's a bit difficult to explain. 'Immanent transcendence' goes beyond the individual and constitutes the group.'

But don't you think it should be possible to see in the various forms of representational space, from classical music to rap or techno, from ancient theater to contemporary art galleries, signs that reveal a conception of the world, and of being-in-the-world, that might constitute new socio-political agency tied to these forms?

Just as today there is something intense and nomadic in being-together, in times when everything was based on representation, there were institutions that came to be fixed. Analogously, I think we can speak of being 'dynamically rooted' and try to show how a particular musical gathering or tribal practice is also an expression of such a dynamic at a time when, to borrow an expression of Ernst Bloch's, there is a 'non-contemporaneity' between what is established and what is still nascent. And this is our own drama, for we in fact continue, with the stock of knowledge we have at our disposition, to function fixed on a thinking about being, and thus have trouble appreciating, in the most basic sense of the word, the dynamic, the recomposition of being-together. This is why intellectuals, whatever the level of their good will, whether left or right, also have trouble appreciating something that is a nascent or dynamic state, because, as I just said, they, too, remain shuttered within a thinking of being. For me, great musical effervescences, raves, for example, do not allow of being apprehended by such thinking, whose concepts prove incapable of comprehending what makes up our present. We think we have grasped them, but they are already elsewhere. Thus, because today being-together is already riven by this dynamic, its forms no longer enfolded into closed and immobile units—this may be where the idea of mixing relates to that of *métissage*, cross-breeding—it is no longer possible to grasp the reality of it with our traditional conceptual instrumentation, which understood being-together only as something fixed and fully rational. For me, this is also related to the failure of the great explanatory systems of modern thought based in individualism, thinking that is more and more paranoid and has no idea what to do next. Whereas we need to figure out how to set up companion structures that will, for the moment, settle for accompanying something in a nascent state.

Is this why you said in Du Nomadisme *that 'the anomic of one moment becomes tomorrow's canonical'[4]?*

It's simply a question of wisdom. When we see what yesterday was considered anomic, we realize it has become the norm. I use this formula to show that in our universities or in our social lives, we make judgments based on something that yesterday was totally anomic. So then, to invert the problem, let us be attentive to what is anomic in the present, not that it will all mechanically somehow become canonical. But conversely, everything that will be canonized is today still on the order of the anomic.

Furthermore, don't raves, and the effervescent and contagious enthusiasm of the dancing in them, along with the participatory experiences being tried in contemporary art, show that the somatic dimension of existence, the body, cannot be limited to the private sphere alone, to the 'minuscule enclosure,' as Bataille called it? Might there not be in fact, rumbling in social space—and in this sense techno would be the the sound and rhythm of that rumbling—something like a resistance, from some imperative need to share, to undergo a collective experience of it?

[4] Ibid.

What was once only a metaphor used by Durkheim, the 'social body,' or as used by other sociologists in a more general way, has here become a reality. I refer you to a line I used in one of my books, I don't remember which, 'The exacerbation of the body proper is a support for the body social.' But of course this social body will not be society as such, but more precisely the little social bodies, the 'tribes': we think like the other, we dress like the other, we screw like the other—a whole series of things that function by imitation. I used that word a moment ago, again from a thinker who was untimely in his own time, but timely in ours, Gabriel Tarde, who spoke of 'laws of imitation.' They were neither true nor relevant in his time, but these 'laws of imitation' at present seem to me particularly conspicuous. To illustrate this proposition, I can cite the paradox of fashion, as formulated by Georg Simmel, even though he didn't think of it as a paradox. He shows how in its beginnings the point of fashion was to distinguish me from the other, to make me singular, whereupon I embark on a paradoxal logic where the sign of distinction spreads, as if by contamination, and tends to be imitated and reproduced. With fashion, while I wish in principle to to separate myself from the other, we curiously find ourselves both looking the same. And that is the idea of fashion, where there is a great paradox. One can see how this working on oneself, this work on the body, tends to sustain a collective body. And this is what leads me to say that the exacerbation of the body proper sustains the body collective.

This goes against the thinking of any number of rather summary approaches to individualism which see in the evolution of the contemporary world nothing but the accentuation of individualism and narcissism. But empirically, what is at work is at most a 'group narcissism,' something that does in fact relate to the development of the person, in the etymological sense of the term, in the roles I play. But there can only be roles if there is a play, something I play with others. I can, of course, like any actor, put the accent on one line of action or another; I exist by reciting my text, but all I do is recite it. It is something that is said, that makes me more said than saying, and even, more acted than acting.

This shows why it is of such interest to note the importance of the body, 'corporism' in all its forms—the body we dress, the body we construct, fashion, dieting, body-building, for example—but also the fact that each of these is done under and for the eye of the other. Even this body I dress, construct and look after is for it to be seen, and I do that under the eye of the other. There is nothing individual or narcissistic about it. Or else we have rethink Narcissus in closer keeping with his myth, as opposed to the way it has been read. He doesn't lose himself in his own image, but is lost or drowned in the pool, which is a metaphor for the world. Here, too, in the myth of Narcissus, we have an element of expenditure—to not fall in love with one's image, but with an image that is in some sense the epitome of the world. And it is in this epitome of the world that Narcissus drowns. It is something on this level that is at stake with the present-day exacerbation of the body.

Just as with the dancing at a rave, when we lose ourselves in a totality, the dancing crowd, which also relates to the lake of Narcissus.

There have been arguments made for the individual dancing we see at raves, where the actor is alone, as opposed to the waltz or the tango, where there are two partners. Even if may practice or appreciate them myself, I find them very simply bourgeois dances with the titanic couple of man and woman, and in the end there is nothing more regimented and boring than that. Whereas in the dimension of collective dancing, there is someone who appears to be isolated, but who can be included in a whole where no distinctions are made between the sexes, and where one may dance before a man or before a woman, or sucessively before a man and a woman. There is also an 'orgiastic' dimension here, one which seems to me much more global, holistic, and, if one may use such a word, 'cosmic,' leading to the possibility of being present at 'loss of self' in the other. For me, contemporary dancing is about this.

Isn't there also an increasingly more urgent need for art to go beyond categories drawn only from the 'fine arts,' the sublime, and the representation of the Idea and Truth, and, as it does so, to remain open to popular culture, and to the festive multiplicities and collective emotion of the bodies that dwell within it? Would this be a way of reviving the festive intensity of traditional societies, for whom art was always festivity, and festivity an art, and who always drew all the arts into the crucible of the fête?

Yes, I totally agree with this observation. This leads me to think that there are no longer separate arts. We can see that the whole 'bourgeoisist' idea of museographical art, apart from life, no longer works very well.

Should we then continue to speak of art? Some people think not, but I think we should. Should we say 'popular arts'? I tend to think so, even though the expression refers to something very specific. We are talking about art that works by capillary action, spreading and diluting into the whole social body, which is also a form of art.

What is 'bourgeoisist' art (from 'bourgeoisism,' which we find in socialism as well as in capitalism)? It is something that stands 'apart'—the dancer for the bourgeois or the museum for the proletarian—and always serves in some way only to allow the reproduction of production, or of labor power. In one sense or the other, it was an art apart, but therefore served—a utilitarian art, or to speak like Heidegger, a 'utensilarian' art.

On the 'popular' side (although I still prefer the notion of art that works by capillary action, which in turn relates to what I meant earlier by 'making one's life into an artwork'), nothing is separate, 'apart.' We are dealing with something which is not on the periphery, but not in the center, either, thus with a totality. In the end, the artist only crystallizes or exacerbates this, saying in his or her own paroxysmal way what theres is to be seen in the *theatrum mundi*, the theater of the street. This is actually a good metaphor for art, which is not 'apart,' but is to be made with those bits of the daily that can be crystallized. This is the image of the genius in the most simple sense of the word: 'genius' depends on having a *gens* [The Roman term for 'clan,' whose guardian spirit was the *genius.—Trans.*] It is a function of the world in which we are situated. It seems to me that we are coming back to this conception of art, to crystallizations, of course, but to rooted ones, organically bound to a given moment.

> *Here we touch upon the status of the artist: does the heroic, sacral, and almost demiurgic status modernity has conferred on the artist somehow make the latter into a pillar of precisely that which makes art into an exercise of sovereignty, thus serving the world of individualism and its ideology? In other words, no longer having any truth or meaning to search for in the abyss (the Romantic attitude) or to represent as the foundation of the community, doesn't the Romantic figure of the sacred artist belong to an age that we are now in the process of leaving behind?*

Anthropologically, in reference to what I just said about the artist, we also come back to the genius, in the sense that there is genius only as a crystallization of something widely lived. There is an image that captures this from Ernst Jünger: that of a splendid crystal, enormous, that was found, while digging the Gotthard Tunnel, but only under the tons of material it takes to produce such a crystal. There is genius—and in any case, this is what seems to me at stake with techno—only through daily artistic practice, through a multiplicity of music groups and artists (even Sunday painters; it's of little importance to the issue) who create a kind of compost. The idea of the qualitative resurfaces here a bit, the idea of art lived on a daily basis, which, of course, here and there crystallizes into notable works. But it is not something separate.

The big difference is that under modernity there is a overweening and mechanical conception, a bit 'exceptionalist,' if you will, of the artist and artwork. Whereas now it's something that to my mind should be analysed in terms of organicity, linking, and liaison in what I call 'dynamic rooting.' This is a term I have used in another domain but which can be applied here: something that has its own momentum, a force in movement, 'in nomadism,' but which at the same time is rooted. This is what is in play in techno—the mixing—and in the practices of contemporary art, whose value lies in the fact that they somehow crystallize the networks in which they are situated. I would say that in every domain, in particular, but not only, in art, the hallmark of modernity was the *primum individuationis*, whereas what seems important to me at present is the *primum relationis*, something whose value lies only in relating, or can only exist because there is relation. Qualitatively, there is an extraordinary difference. It is all too easy to speak of an epistemological break, but there really is one between the *primum individuationis* and the *primum relationis*.

Thus, unlike some people, I continue to think that art is still possible. But no longer a 'separate' art—that remains just art. A 'rooted' art, art in liaison.

In your book Au Creux des apparences (In the Hollow of Appearances), *you say that for post-modern esthetics, the value of the 'trivial object' or the art-object lies both in itself and in the relation it establishes or favors. It is no longer a relation to Meaning or the Ideal that is in the forefront, but its capacity for relating. To the extent that art no longer dispenses Meaning, Truth, or the One and Only, but on the contrary presents itself as their suspension and fragmentation (you used the term 'fractalization'), does it not provide reasons, if not the reason, for the rejection of contemporary art, as well as for the 'quarrel' or polemic linked to it?*

I must admit I find it a somewhat abstract polemic, rather 'Parisian,' in the negative sense of the word. I don't see much point in it, for it derives from a notion that continues an analysis of art based on categories that are in sum very 'modern,' and on a critique of 'modernity' that is now inoperative. 'There is still art or there is nothing,' roughly speaking. The positions are so uncompromising, yet nonetheless, as in lock-jaw, hold each other in place. In the end, it's like an old couple unable to separate, who stays together despite the conjugal warfare. Something like that is in play in the art 'quarrel.' We must find another line of attack and a way out. That's what I was trying to point out when I said all that remains to be said is that anything can be an art-form. Then even kitsch could be one. Abraham Moles proved as much, in his own way, using the gnomes and wells people put in their gardens in the suburbs of Lorraine. We can think about all kinds of things, even within the midst of the banal. I prefer to take this line of attack, showing even there, up to and including the banal, there is something which is artistic.

In this regard, I would simply repeat, since 'daily life' was the subject of my first books, that the word 'banal,' which now means 'nothing' or 'flat,' goes back to the expression 'day of the banal oven,' the day the lord lost control of his oven and had to cede the right to use it to anyone, even serfs. It was also the feast-day of the common bread, also beyond the control of the overbearing, in this case the lords. It is a bit curious that we have taken this feast-day to mean something that is 'nothing.' But on reflection, we can show that in this 'nothing' there is 'everything.' And it is in this nothing—here we come back to Bataille, and to Eastern philosophy, where the hollow is the 'hole,' that is, the vagina—that, in various modulations, originates what, in substance, gives life. I think there is in banality something like a womb, the cup and cut from which existence emerges. This is how we should be posing the problem, instead of holding on to this quarrel whether 'There still is. . . There isn't any more. . . ,' with all the possible declensions of contemporary art or the position that art today doesn't mean much. I myself prefer to take a tangent on this issue; I would leave the two opposing camps of the quarrel back to back, or face to face, if you wish, and try to recover a much more, in my mind, lively dimension of life, much more incarnate, and, I dare say, much more real, one which does not recognize itself in representational forms, for or against, but quite simply affirms itself. Here, too, let us go back to Nietzsche: not to the No, but to the affirmative thought, the 'song of the Yes.' There is in daily life, in the banal, this song of the 'Yes' that crystallizes into art.

Isn't there, somewhere on the horizon of our existence, and of art, too, a 'cosmological revolution' (of which techno may be a precursor), in that the new virtual universes generated in and by the development of new technologies are no longer a representation or copy of the real, but something like a prolongation or augmentation of it, in turn giving rise to new sensibilities, as well as to a new way of being-in-body and being-in-the-world and sharing it?

I think that what you are saying relates to going beyond that great and pure dichotomy which so marked modernity. There was the real and unreal; things that were true and things that were false; what was image and what wasn't, etc. There is a whole iconoclastic tradition in the Western tradition, whose roots we see in the Bible and its subsequent concretization and philosophical canonization in Descartes, and which is constantly to be found, with the exception of a few authors like Merleau-Ponty, both as a fear of the image and in the fact that we think the real is rational, and that therefore only what is tangible is real. We then come to realize, and the work of Gilbert Durand has in his own way demonstrated as much, that we can only 'understand the real,' speaking like Max Weber, from the unreal.

Henceforth, for example, the virtual is no longer the opposite of the real, as if were something phantasmal. But the virtual, here in its most simple, almost Aristotelian, sense, is itself just another modulation of the real. In German there is a distinction made between *Realität* and *Wirklichkeit*, the latter being that on which we are founded, that which is tangible; this alone was recognized as being real. But the German philosophers who made the distinction demonstrated that *Realität* was a 'sur-real' that somehow integrates the real. I would say there is something like this at work in the practice of the image, the imaginary, the present-day 'imaginal world,' which leads us to feed on the immaterial, and also to feed, in the most simple sense of the word, on the symbolic dimensions of existence which unite me to the world and unite me to others.

Henri Corbin, inspired by German philosophy, spoke, applying it to Iranian Sufis, of the 'imaginal world,' that is, to a world intermediate between the macrocosmos and the earthly. We can use this idea of the 'imaginal world' to show how the image, too, is a milieu, middle, and medium between the micro- and macrocosmos, the latter being social life. There is, thus, in the image something that binds—binds us to the surrounding world, and also to the social environment—a communial and eucharistic notion, the sharing of images. But here I differ—though God knows I was inspired by them—from the Situationists. Let's just say I differ from an excessively catechetical or dogmatic reading of the world of the spectacle, and of the society of the spectacle, as being constitutionally alienating. I think that, on the contrary, we should go back to the image in its virtual aspect, and in its real one, as being a form of liaison, of bonding, to the other, to otherness. I see alterity in three terms: the other of the small group (for me the 'tribe'); the alterity and the other of Nature (I am linked to Nature by virtue of the image, since the image has a sensible aspect, a natural, almost naturalistic, one); and to the Other of God, of deity, whatever deity may mean). To designate this more clearly I shall borrow a term from Gilbert Durand which I often use, the 'mesocosmic image,' from 'meso-cosmos,' the world of the middle, in the sense that it is what once again unites me to the various forms of alterity, whether it be the other of the tribe, of Nature, or of the deity. I think the image really does have this communial function; it is not a negation of the world or of sociality. It is something that, on the contrary, truly helps sustain alterity.

Don't you think all these political, technical, and artistic transformations, as we have seen and experienced them in techno, attest to a more global upheaval of our world, as if the change we were witnessing were not merely one of degree or in the status of our Western civilization, but more profoundly a true change of kind, one that might bring it to an end, or lead to its exhaustion? Does this open onto something else, another world, where art (in the sense of the Greek techné) *might replace politics as a means of singular and collective invention of our existences?*

Yes. Your observation is a kind of précis of everything that has been said so far. Obviously, if we use the word 'politics' in its most simple sense, that is, as a 'project,' in the way the great political scientist Julien Freund defined it so well, showing that fundamentally the political is always something that relates to this idea of the distant, an end or goal to be attained. What seems to me most striking is that there is no longer a project to speak of. But there is this idea of the 'present,' the idea of enjoying the 'here and now,' everything we previously said about the

'qualitative,' what I have been trying trying to say about the 'presentation' of the world, and about the dynamic element there is in the order of
the world. Yet it is difficult to say whether we are now passing into
another world. It is certain, if I want to try and be specific, that just as
there was a Westernization of the world in the nineteenth century, there
is a contemporary form of 'Easternization.' It should be understood that
when I say this I don't mean an Orientalization by some particular
Orient over there, but mythical Orients, that is, post-modern ones. We
are witnessing the liaison and convergence of various fragments of the
Far East, South America, Africa, and Europe and, in keeping with the
image of a post-modernist edifice made up of various quotations, as the
architects of the '50s might say, a post-modernity made up of Orients,
and expressed in the religious, philosophical, and everyday syncretisms
we can see around us.

The common denominator of this patchwork of Orients is the
'present.' We have already emphasized 'presentation' and 'presentifica-
tion.' Perhaps we can end by recalling the meaning of the word 'present,'
which is not just something static, the acceptance of the status quo
without moving, the opposite of a politics that is trying to save the
world. There is more of the 'being before oneself' about it (that is the
meaning of the Latin *præsens*). The very notion of 'present' closes the
short-circuit I described earlier with respect to 'rootedness.' There is
indeed a being that is there ('I live with others here and now,' *Carpe
diem*' ['Seize the day'], the qualitative aspect of existence), yet at the same
time there is an internal force in that present. So then we are dealing not
with a finalized reason, a reason that tends toward a goal, one which, as
Adorno argued, all of nineteenth-century rationalism was based, but
neither is it irrationalism. This demonstrates an 'interior reason' in the
present, a 'ratio-vitalism'[5]

Thus all situations have a reason proper to them. This is quite striking,
for this is what is being experienced today in great popular gatherings like
techno parties. Once again, it all goes back to this eternal present, that is, a
present that is at once dynamic and rooted.

---

[5] cf. Michel Maffesoli, *Éloge de la raison sensible* [*In Praise of Sensible Reason*], Grasset, Paris,
1996

Also available from Dis Voir

ÉDITIONS DIS VOIR : 3, RUE BEAUTREILLIS – F-75004 PARIS
TÉLÉPHONE (33) 01 48 87 07 09 – FAX (33) 01 48 87 07 14
e-mail: DISVOIR@AOL.com